Microsoft Dynamics AX 2012 Financial Management

Get to grips with how to successfully use Microsoft Dynamics AX 2012 for financial management with this concise and practical reference guide

Mohamed Aamer

[PACKT] enterprise

PUBLISHING

professional expertise distilled

BIRMINGHAM - MUMBAI

Microsoft Dynamics AX 2012 Financial Management

First published: November 2013

Production Reference: 1151113

Published by Packt Publishing Ltd.
Livery Place
35 Livery Street
Birmingham B3 2PB, UK.

ISBN 978-1-78217-720-3

www.packtpub.com

Cover Image by Aniket Sawant (aniket_sawant_photography@hotmail.com)

Credits

Author

Mohamed Aamer

Reviewers

Kamalakannan Elangovan

Wim Vanhoorne

Acquisition Editors

Llewellyn Rozario

Gregory Wild

Commissioning Editor

Manasi Pandire

Technical Editors

Rosmy George

Ankita Thakur

Copy Editors

Deepti Kapadia

Lavina Pereira

Gladson Monteiro

Aditya Nair

Project Coordinator

Suraj Bist

Proofreader

Ameesha Green

Indexer

Priya Subramani

Graphics

Sheetal Aute

Ronak Dhruv

Valentina Dsilva

Yuvraj Mannari

Production Coordinator

Manu Joseph

Cover Work

Manu Joseph

About the Author

Mohamed Aamer is a Microsoft Dynamics AX Support Engineer for EMEA region with Microsoft, Egypt. In 2013, he was awarded Microsoft Dynamics AX MVP, and is the first AX MVP in the Middle East and Africa. His main focus is on implementing Microsoft Dynamics AX to fit customers' needs. He uses his time to understand customer business cycles and solve customer business problems through a combination of business process re-engineering and utilization of the application functionalities. He is a Microsoft Certified Professional (MCP) specialized in financial management and supply chain management. In addition to this, he is a Microsoft Certified Trainer (MCT).

Mohamed has varied consultation experience in dealing with Microsoft Golden Partners and Microsoft customers. He has worked as a consultant in many industries such as Retail Fashion, Retail Electronics, Cement Manufacturing, Trading, and Ready Mix. He has carried out multiple implementations of Microsoft Dynamics Retail Management System and Microsoft Dynamics AX in numerous capacities, such as Project Manager, Solutions Architect, and Lead Consultant. His consulting skills are complemented by his business, management, and interpersonal skills.

He is also a column author of AX-Excellence at MSDynamicsWorld.com community, an official blogger at Microsoft Dynamics Community, and a blogger on his own blog www.blog.mohamedaamer.com. He delivers evangelizing sessions to Microsoft Student Partners (MSPs) to introduce Microsoft Dynamics AX and Microsoft Dynamics Sure Step to them. He has been ranked in the top 100 influential people in DynamicsWorld.co.uk for two consecutive years. He has obtained other badges from Microsoft, such as Microsoft Community Contributor (MCC) and Microsoft Dynamics Community Expert.

When not working on complex business processes, he attends live Sufi shows and music concerts.

Acknowledgments

My sincere thanks to all the people who directly/indirectly taught, guided, supported, and advised me to become a consultant. I am doing my best to improve myself. This acknowledgment is for the people who have made a massive impact on my career. I'd like to thank all of them as I cannot thank them enough.

I dedicate this book to the memory of my father and my uncle Hamza; both of them invested in my brother and myself the seed of concepts and beliefs and now we are harvesting them. My father always said to me, "I believe in you when you say you can do; you can achieve more than what you target, just focus", and my uncle Hamza said to me after my graduation, "You just met your lifetime teacher who will guide you through your entire life".

My older brother Ramy, who is my inspiration, gives me his time, effort, daily advice, coaching, and leadership. He always gives me support and encourages me. He is my mentor. Ramy put me on the Information Technology track and gave me the chance to choose which gate I will pass through. He helped me to finish my college and convinced me to attend the first e-commerce seminar in the Middle East; that was the first spark. I consider Ramy as my source of energy.

I cannot forget my mother's support and her prayers for me.

Also, my wife sacrificed so much of our personal life during the development of my career, and I cannot thank her enough for that.

Dr. Salah El Kashef is the Corporate Training and Consulting Director — Middle East and North Africa Region Governors Consulting Services, LLC. Salah was my first instructor who introduced the e-commerce subject to me in 2002 and helped me become a certified e-commerce consultant before my graduation. He helped me by directing my career to Information Technology Management.

Shaimaa Farid is an IT Administrator at The Alexandria Trust. I have worked with her as an application consultant for Microsoft Dynamics RMS. She is the one who provided me with information on an opportunity to take up Microsoft Dynamics AX scholarship in 2008 with Microsoft. She provides a lot of support and encouragement to me to focus on my career as a consultant. Shaimaa is one of the best customer-oriented people I have worked with.

Mohamed Samy is a Chief Technology Officer. He is the one who introduced me to the community as a speaker at Cairo Code Camp. I used to deliver sessions with him as a co-presenter evangelizing Microsoft Dynamics AX and Microsoft Dynamics Sure Step to the Egyptian community. He predicted that I will be an AX MVP. He is a very talented IT geek with unique creative solutions. I enjoy our community activities together.

Ahmed Abuelmaged is an Academic Developer Evangelist with Microsoft. He used to manage and schedule the Microsoft Dynamics AX and Microsoft Dynamics Sure Step sessions with Microsoft Student Partners (MSPs). I believe we did a good job, especially when I see students joining that field.

Ahmed Kazem is a Development consultant. He is an artistic developer. He can absorb any technology in a very short time. He is the one who develops, maintains, and supports my blog technically. I have never met a smart and gifted developer like him.

Dr. Nezar Samy is the Director of Information Systems Department, Nile University. He was my instructor for Information Technology Management Professional Certificate at America University in Cairo. He taught me the perspective of the IT role as a business enabler, and gave me a chance to improve my presentation skills.

Chandru Chankar is an EMEA & LATAM ERP Lead with Microsoft. He has given me a lot of motivation and support during my career. I can always approach him for an advice and to share ideas. I am very proud to meet a person like him and consider him as a family friend. He is my career role model.

Jason Gumpert is the Editor of MSDynamicsWorld.com. I have been working with him since 2012 as an author for my featured column in the MSDynamicsWorld community. He gave me the chance to advance my writing technique and style, from blogging to writing articles. I believe my articles will reach more people through his community. He is an open-minded person and is always open to new initiatives.

Ashraf Abusen is a Group Financial Controller with ASEC Cement. He coached me to understand the logical thinking of building a practical solution for real business practices, and how to streamline the offered solution with all business divisions. He is a charismatic leader. He has the sense of building the iterative road map of the ERP solution.

Ashraf Aly is a Global ERP Director for Ascom Network Testing. He is a talented manager who can manage and drive complex ERP implementations. He spotted my skills and gave me the opportunity to utilize my abilities and show it up. He has a unique flexibility technique to deal with stakeholders of the project and to achieve the objectives. Julie Gale is a Project Manager with Microsoft.She helped me to learn more about Microsoft Dynamics Sure Step. She also supported me in community activities.

Microsoft Dynamics Academic Alliance team: Ashley Pecoraro, the Program Manager for Academic Alliance Team at Microsoft, and Lyndsey Creamer, Program Manager/ Project Manager for the Microsoft Dynamics Academic Alliance team at Microsoft. Ashley and Lyndsey gave me a lot of support, while I was involved with Microsoft Dynamics Academic Alliance, so I could share my knowledge and experience for their members. They are very open to ideas, and they are willing to help as far as they can.

Microsoft Dynamics Community team that includes Nick Hoban, Sr. Release Manager ECIT at Microsoft. He guided me in the right direction to share my blog posts with the Dynamics Community.

Microsoft Dynamics AX—MVPs: Brandon George, Microsoft MVP and Director of Business Intelligence at Sunrise Technologies; Fred Chen, Development Manager at Systems Advisers Group, Australia; and Antonio Gilabert, Microsoft Dynamics AX MVP Founder at AX3, gave me a lot of support and encouragement as an MVP. They are enriching the community with their experience and knowledge around Microsoft Dynamics AX.

About the Reviewers

Kamalakannan Elangovan started his career in 2005 as a technical consultant in ERP for Sonata, where he played a key role in the development of Business Integration solutions for Microsoft. He later moved on to become the head the Business Integration Development team. He spearheaded the development of a commodity trading vertical for a UK-based ISV. It was during this experience that he picked up his passion for product development. And this passion has driven his career since then.

In 2008, Kamal joined InnoVites and lead the product development of InnoVites, creating one of the first vertical for Dynamics AX on multidimensional industry such as cables and wires. Currently, he works with Curogens as a Development Manager overseeing product development efforts. As a Microsoft Dynamics AX enthusiast and architect, he shares his insights by contributing to the Microsoft Dynamics community through his blog, `http://kamalblogs.wordpress.com`.

> I would like to thank Packt Publishing and the author for offering me the chance to review and read this wonderful book. It has been a great learning experience doing so.

Wim Vanhoorne, a formal Operation manager in a project-oriented production industry, started his first AXAPTA (original name of Dynamics AX) implementation in 1999.

This was the start of a large number of successful implementations around the world in different business sectors as a program manager, cross-functional consultant, and solution architect. Wim, certified in Microsoft Dynamics AX, built a solid knowledge of all the functional and technical aspects of Microsoft Dynamics AX.

Currently, he is working as a program manager for an international construction company responsible for functional and development teams, along with everything required to deliver large-scale Dynamics AX implementations.

www.PacktPub.com

Support files, eBooks, discount offers and more

You might want to visit www.PacktPub.com for support files and downloads related to your book.

Did you know that Packt offers eBook versions of every book published, with PDF and ePub files available? You can upgrade to the eBook version at www.PacktPub.com and as a print book customer, you are entitled to a discount on the eBook copy. Get in touch with us at service@packtpub.com for more details.

At www.PacktPub.com, you can also read a collection of free technical articles, sign up for a range of free newsletters and receive exclusive discounts and offers on Packt books and eBooks.

http://PacktLib.PacktPub.com

Do you need instant solutions to your IT questions? PacktLib is Packt's online digital book library. Here, you can access, read and search across Packt's entire library of books.

Why Subscribe?

- Fully searchable across every book published by Packt
- Copy and paste, print and bookmark content
- On demand and accessible via web browser

Free Access for Packt account holders

If you have an account with Packt at www.PacktPub.com, you can use this to access PacktLib today and view nine entirely free books. Simply use your login credentials for immediate access.

Instant Updates on New Packt Books

Get notified! Find out when new books are published by following @PacktEnterprise on Twitter, or the *Packt Enterprise* Facebook page.

Table of Contents

Preface

The essential foundation of the **enterprise resource planning** (**ERP**) implementation is the financial part, which is considered as the backbone of the implementation. The implementation team from the partner's side and the customer's side should ensure that the financial module is well-structured and designed. This book provides a broad guide to Microsoft Dynamics AX 2012 Financial Management fundamentals for all parties involved in the implementation project, with considerations on the business rationale behind functions, basic setups, configurations, transactions on action, and a mention of real-life scenarios.

What this book covers

Chapter 1, *Understanding the General Ledger*, explains the usage of main accounts, control points, and the Microsoft Dynamics AX 2012 shared financial data concept. It also gives practical insights into opening balance tips and the month-end closing procedure.

Chapter 2, *Understanding Cash and Bank Management*, will help you understand the integration of the cash and bank management module and their controls, and will conclude with the bank reconciliation process.

Chapter 3, *Functioning of Cash Flow Management*, covers the integration points between cash flow management and other modules in Microsoft Dynamics AX 2012, provided with basic setups, configuration, and cash flow transaction.

Chapter 4, *Working with Cost Management*, covers the inventory costing model in Microsoft Dynamics AX 2012, providing information about inventory cost setups and configuration, recalculation, and closing.

Chapter 5, *Exploring Financial Dimensions*, helps you discover the Microsoft Dynamics AX 2012 financial dimensions model, the practical utilization of financial dimension, and its reporting.

Chapter 6, Exploring Financial Reporting and Analysis, helps you to find out the reporting needs at early stages of the implementation project, and the factors you should consider during the project life cycle. We discuss Microsoft Dynamics AX 2012 inquiry forms and the **SQL Server Reporting Services** (**SSRS**) reports.

What you need for this book

All the examples can be done using a virtual machine of Microsoft Dynamics AX 2012 R2 Image from the Microsoft partner/customer source.

Who this book is for

This book is designed for newcomers to business solutions, as well as experienced practitioners getting into the Microsoft Dynamics AX 2012 field. If you are involved in one or more of the roles stated below, then this book is for you:

- **Customer side**: Chief financial officer, financial controller, accounting manager, subject matter expert, power user, key user, business analyst, business decision maker, and chief information officer.

- **Partner side**: Solution architect, application consultant, project manager, support engineer, Pre-technical Sales Consultant, and account manager.

Conventions

In this book, you will find a number of styles of text that distinguish between different kinds of information. Here are some examples of these styles and an explanation of their meaning.

New terms and **important words** are shown in bold. Words that you see on the screen, in menus or dialog boxes for example, appear in the text like this: "For main accounts' type, navigate to **General ledger** | **Setup** | **Chart of accounts** | **Chart of accounts**."

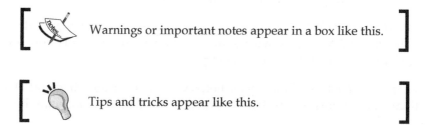

Warnings or important notes appear in a box like this.

Tips and tricks appear like this.

Reader feedback

Feedback from our readers is always welcome. Let us know what you think about this book—what you liked or may have disliked. Reader feedback is important for us to develop titles that you really get the most out of.

To send us general feedback, simply send an e-mail to feedback@packtpub.com, and mention the book title via the subject of your message.

If there is a topic that you have expertise in and you are interested in either writing or contributing to a book, see our author guide on www.packtpub.com/authors.

Customer support

Now that you are the proud owner of a Packt book, we have a number of things to help you to get the most from your purchase.

Errata

Although we have taken every care to ensure the accuracy of our content, mistakes do happen. If you find a mistake in one of our books—maybe a mistake in the text or the code—we would be grateful if you would report this to us. By doing so, you can save other readers from frustration and help us improve subsequent versions of this book. If you find any errata, please report them by visiting http://www.packtpub.com/submit-errata, selecting your book, clicking on the **errata submission form** link, and entering the details of your errata. Once your errata are verified, your submission will be accepted and the errata will be uploaded on our website, or added to any list of existing errata, under the Errata section of that title. Any existing errata can be viewed by selecting your title from http://www.packtpub.com/support.

Piracy

Piracy of copyright material on the Internet is an ongoing problem across all media. At Packt, we take the protection of our copyright and licenses very seriously. If you come across any illegal copies of our works, in any form, on the Internet, please provide us with the location address or website name immediately so that we can pursue a remedy.

Please contact us at copyright@packtpub.com with a link to the suspected pirated material.

We appreciate your help in protecting our authors, and our ability to bring you valuable content.

Questions

You can contact us at `questions@packtpub.com` if you are having a problem with any aspect of the book, and we will do our best to address it.

1
Understanding the General Ledger

The **chart of accounts (COA)** is the backbone of **enterprise resource planning** (ERP). It is a part of the financial module, which is the foundational module of ERP. It is a list of categorized ledger accounts (known as main accounts in Microsoft Dynamics AX 2012 R2) that is used by the organization to record all financial transactions, and it depends on the nature of the organization's business. The chart of accounts of manufacturing companies differs from trading companies, service companies, and so on. This chapter covers the following topics:

- Understanding the chart of accounts
- Classifying main accounts
- Controlling main accounts
- Understanding shared financial data
- Understanding financial management in action
- Opening balance
- Performing daily transactions
- Closing procedure

Understanding the chart of accounts

The classified skeleton of a main account is the responsibility of the controller from the customer side and the application consultant from the partner side, who bridges the application capabilities to the customers' requirements. This activity is designed in the analysis and design phases, and deployed in the deployment phase.

The main accounts are at the core of financial reporting, and include the trial balance, balance sheet, income statement, working capital, and cash flow. The starting point in building COAs is identifying the financial reporting requirements to ensure all classification levels and categories are captured in Microsoft Dynamics AX.

Classifying main accounts

The first classification of main accounts in Microsoft Dynamics AX is the type, which represents the nature of the ledger account; that is, is it a balance sheet account or a profit and loss account. The following diagram shows an example of a balance sheet and an income statement:

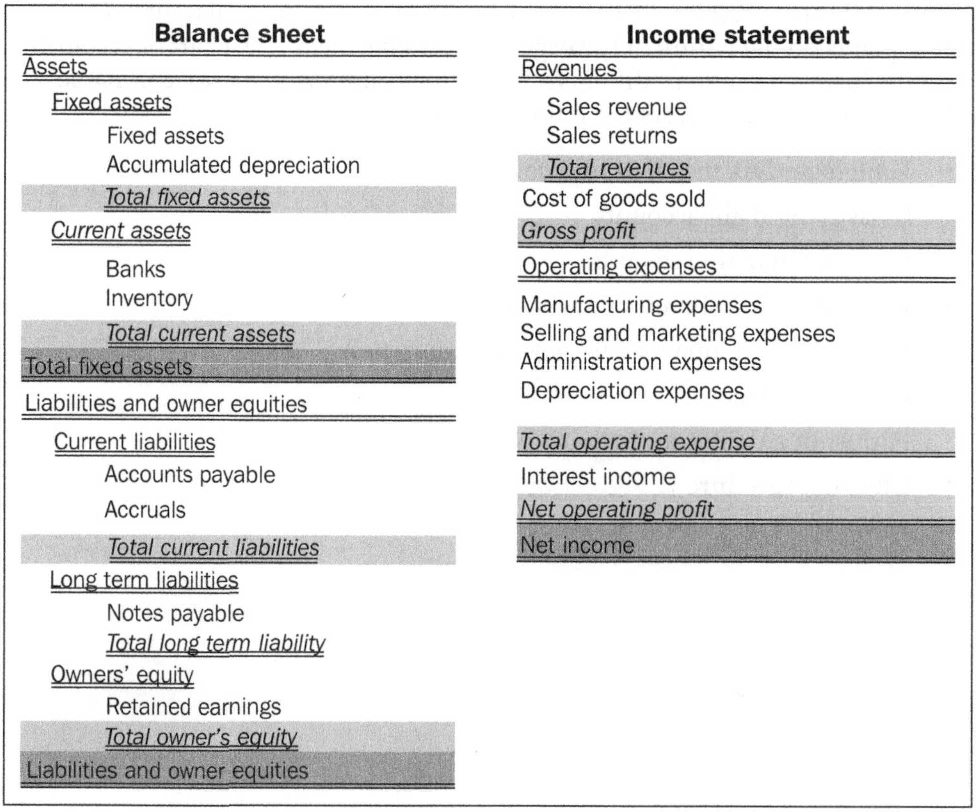

Balance sheet	Income statement
Assets	**Revenues**
Fixed assets	Sales revenue
Fixed assets	Sales returns
Accumulated depreciation	*Total revenues*
Total fixed assets	Cost of goods sold
Current assets	*Gross profit*
Banks	Operating expenses
Inventory	Manufacturing expenses
Total current assets	Selling and marketing expenses
Total fixed assets	Administration expenses
Liabilities and owner equities	Depreciation expenses
Current liabilities	*Total operating expense*
Accounts payable	Interest income
Accruals	*Net operating profit*
Total current liabilities	Net income
Long term liabilities	
Notes payable	
Total long term liability	
Owners' equity	
Retained earnings	
Total owner's equity	
Liabilities and owner equities	

Microsoft Dynamics AX classifies main account types into two main groups. The first group is **Transactional accounts**, where all financial transactions are recorded. The second group is **Reporting** accounts, which is used for reporting and classifying caption totals.

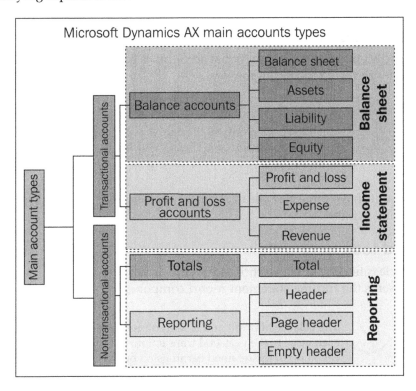

The transactional accounts that carry posted transactions on the application maintain a record of all the data related to the transaction. This includes the main account number, amount, transaction side (debit/credit), currency, transaction text, and transaction type, in addition to original documents (which generate this entry), and who posted the transaction.

These classifications help at the reporting level and are considered as the first classification layer for main accounts.

In order to view all the main account types, navigate to **General ledger | Setup | Chart of accounts | Chart of accounts**. You can double-click on **Main account** or click on **Edit** and then on the **General** tab. Another option is to navigate to **General ledger | Common | Main accounts**. You can also double-click on **Main account** or click on **Edit** and then on the **General** tab.

Using transactional accounts

Transactional accounts represent the primary classification of the main accounts. They are divided into two main groups: the first is **Balance accounts** and the second is **Profit and loss accounts**.

Balance accounts

The first classification type of transactional accounts is balance accounts, which represent balance sheet report components.

> The balance in a balance account is calculated from the account-opening day till the date of reporting. In the year-end transaction, the closing voucher is transferred to the opening balance of the account.

Balance accounts have three classifications that represent their nature: **Assets**, **Liabilities**, and **Equity**.

Profit and loss accounts

The second classification of transactional accounts is profit and loss accounts, which represents the **Income statement** report components.

> The balance of profit and loss accounts are reset to zero each year. In the year-end transaction, the balances are rolled up in the retained earnings account.

As you can see in the following screenshot, profit and loss accounts have three classifications that represent the nature of accounts: **Profit and loss**, **Expense**, and **Revenue**:

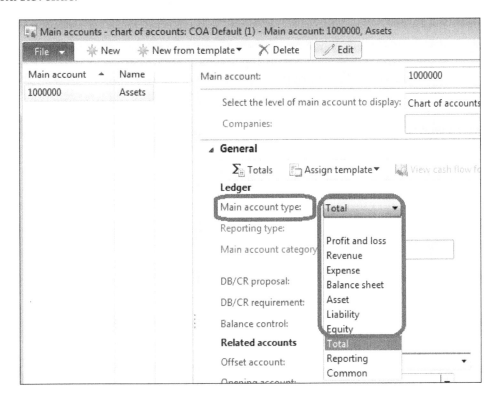

Using nontransactional accounts

Nontransactional accounts represent the financial reporting presentation, which is divided into two main types: **Totals** and **Reporting**. No transactions are allowed to be posted on these accounts.

Totals

Totals are used to sum up the caption or subcaption range of main accounts to give a quick overview of the account's balance, as shown in the following screenshot:

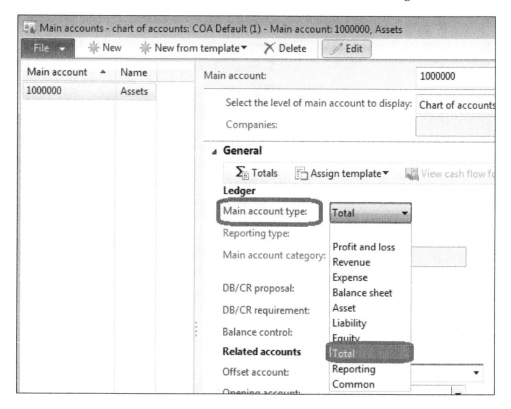

The total of accounts is managed through an account interval form in order to identify the range of total.

If there are subtotal accounts, they are neglected in the grand total. Do not worry — there are no duplications in the calculation of totals.

Reporting

The **Reporting type:** dropdown is used to manage the presentation of financial reporting. The available options are **Header**, **Empty header**, and **Page header**, as shown in the following screenshot:

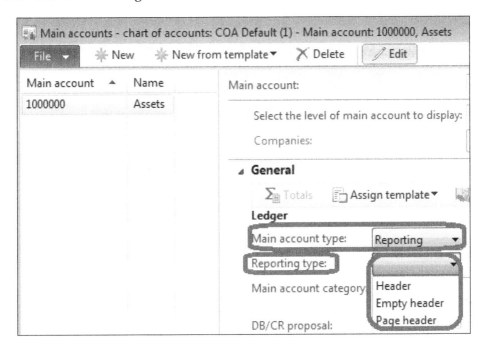

Main account categories

Main account categories represent a second level of classification and are used as a grouping layer for the main accounts.

 More than fifty ledger account categories are provided by default.

In order to view all the main account categories, navigate to **General ledger | Setup | Chart of accounts | Main account categories**. The following screenshot shows the main account categories screen:

> If the **Closed** checkbox is marked, that particular **Reference ID** cannot be selected in the main account form. It is better to serialize the reference IDs in the logical order of reporting levels so that they can be used as a sorting identifier.

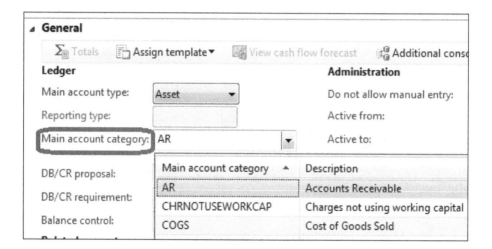

Controlling the main accounts

As seen in the following diagram, Microsoft Dynamics AX offers three main groups of controls over the main accounts. The first is specific to debit and credit controls, the second to account administration, and the third to posting validation.

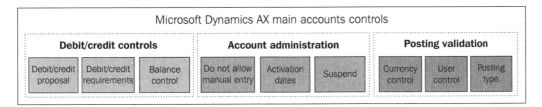

Debit/credit controls

The **Debit/credit controls** group is divided into three subgroups: the first is **Debit/credit proposal**, the second is **Debit/credit requirements**, and the third is **Balance control**.

Debit/credit proposal

Every main account has a normal accounting side, be it debit or credit. The financial controller may prefer to have Microsoft Dynamics AX suggest to accountants the side of account (whether it is debit or credit) as a proposal and give the user the option to move to the other side according to the transaction. This is recommended for accountants with experience.

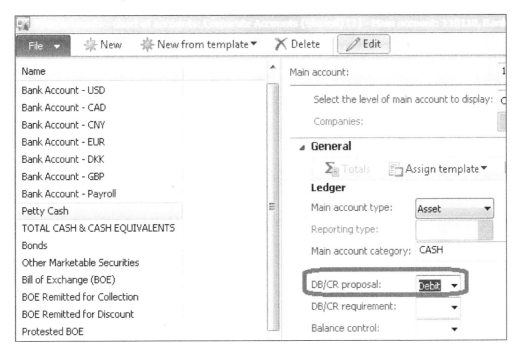

During the processing of a transaction, the cursor moves to the side that is configured in the debit/credit proposal (when the *Tab* key is pressed) as shown in the following screenshot:

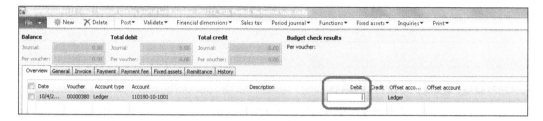

Debit/credit requirements

Every main account has a normal accounting balance, be it debit or credit, and this main account may be debited or credited. The financial controller may prefer to get Microsoft Dynamics AX to control specific main accounts in order to prevent end users from shifting the entry side of the main account. The following screenshot shows the debit/credit requirements of a main account:

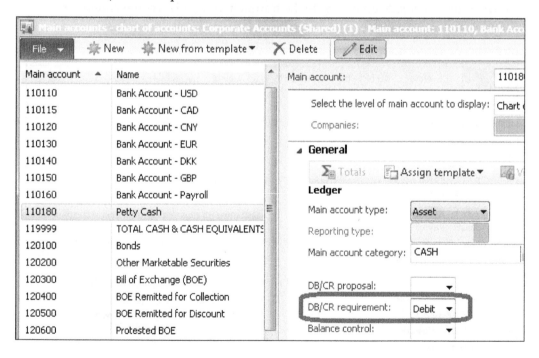

The main account configuration is **Debit**. The accountant attempts to enter transactions in the credit side, as you can see in the following screenshot:

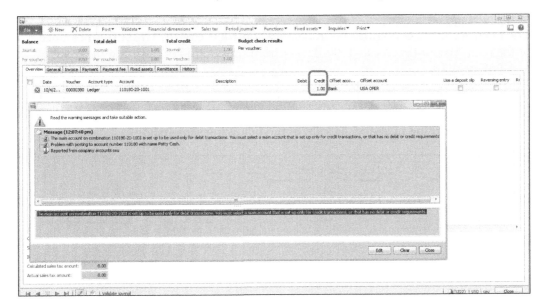

Balance control

Every main account has a normal accounting side, be it debit or credit. If the balance contradicts this norm, it indicates a concern and should be outlined. The financial controller may have preferences to get Microsoft Dynamics AX to control a specific main account's balance in order to prevent any balance issues.

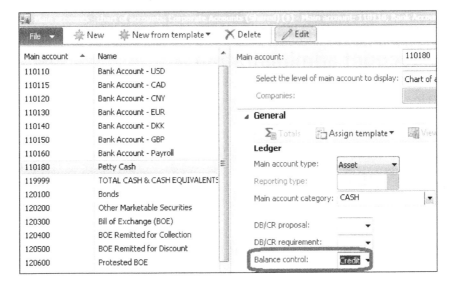

If the balance control is broken during the processing of a transaction, an **Infolog** will pop up: **A requirement for credit balance is selected for account #####, but this is violated by voucher #.##**.

The main account's configuration in balance control is **Credit**. The current balance of the main account is credit -1000. The current transaction is crediting the main account by -1001.

While posting the entry, Microsoft Dynamics AX certifies the main account's balance control configuration and then calculates the current balance. The difference is shown in an **Infolog** message, as seen in the following screenshot:

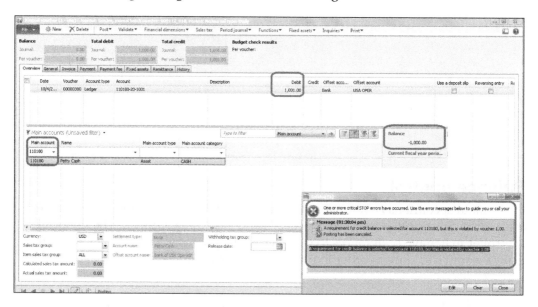

Using account administration

The main account administration is divided into three main groups. The first group is **Do not allow manual entry**, the second is **Date activation**, and the third is **Accounts suspension**.

Do not allow manual entry

The integrity between the general ledger and subledger is an essential factor in ERP. It is characterized in the main accounts and subledgers. The subledger should guarantee that all posted transactions to the general ledger are from the submodules' end. Microsoft Dynamics AX controls the main accounts; this does not allow any direct transactions to be posted to the main account. This means that any transaction affecting a main account must be posted throughout the submodules posting profile. This checkbox is **Do not Allow Manual Entry**, which was known as **Locked in Journal** in Microsoft Dynamics AX 2009.

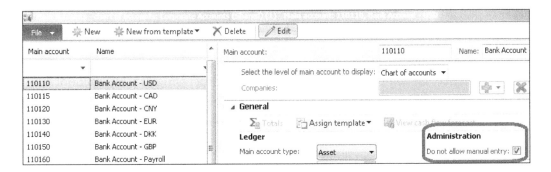

During the processing of a transaction; if an accountant wants to select a main account and this account is configured as **Do not allow manual entry**, an **Infolog** will pop up: **Value (account ####) is not allowed for manual entry. Enter another value**, as shown in the following screenshot:

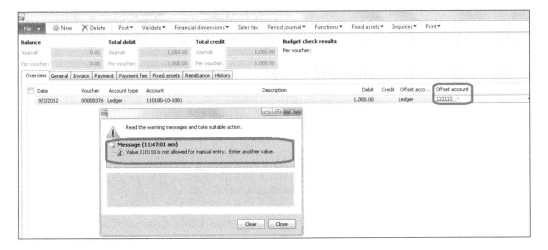

Activation date

The activation date is commonly used for newly created accounts (which will be active for operations at a future date) and in another scenario for main accounts (which may be deactivated after a specific period), as shown in the following screenshot:

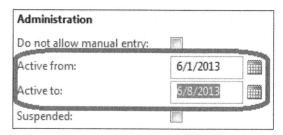

If an accountant wants to work with a main account but it is not a day when the account is active, an **Infolog** will pop up during the processing of a transaction: **Main account ###### is not active**, as shown in the following screenshot:

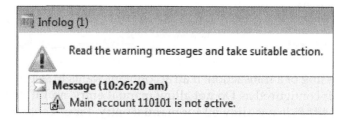

Suspending account

As seen in the following screenshot, there is a control to suspend an account from operational posting:

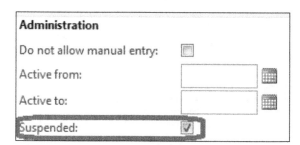

During the processing of a transaction; if an accountant selects a main account that is suspended, an **Infolog** will pop up: **Main account ###### is closed**, as shown in the following screenshot:

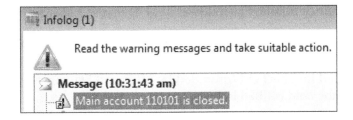

Using posting validation

Posting validation is divided into three main groups. The first group is currency control, the second is user control, and the third is posting type control.

Currency control

The financial controller may prefer to get Microsoft Dynamics AX to control specific currencies in order to stop transactions in other currencies in the main account.

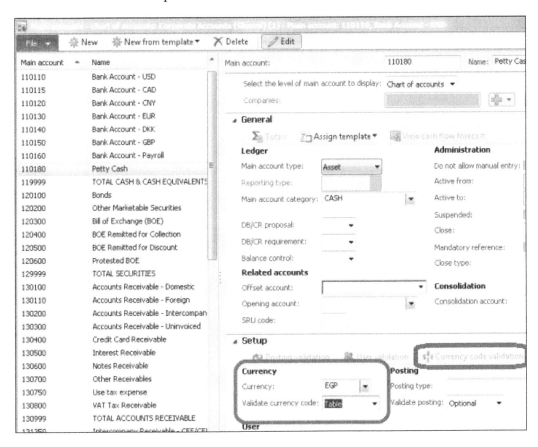

The validation code options are as follows:

- **Optional**: This field is not authenticated at the time of posting. This is the default setting.

- **To be filled in**: This field (provided by Microsoft Dynamics AX) checks whether the field is filled in for posting.

- **Table**: This field (provided by Microsoft Dynamics AX) examines whether the field is completed for posting, and that the value matches the value specified in the main account.

- **List**: This field verifies that the field is filled in with one of the values that are defined on the **Validation list** button.

 Currency code validation is only activated if the selected validation is a list.

During the processing of a transaction; if an accountant changes the currency, an **Infolog** will pop up: **The currency must be EGP for account ######**, as shown in the following screenshot:

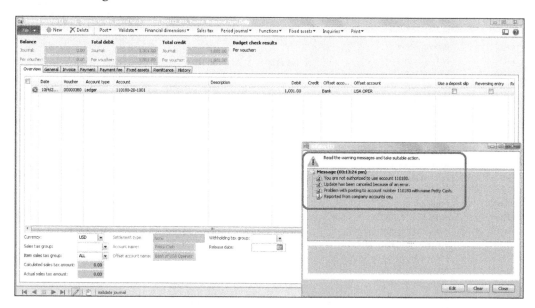

User control

Every main account might have a posting constraint per user. The financial controller may prefer to get Microsoft Dynamics AX to control specific accounts for certain end users who are permitted to post transactions on these main accounts.

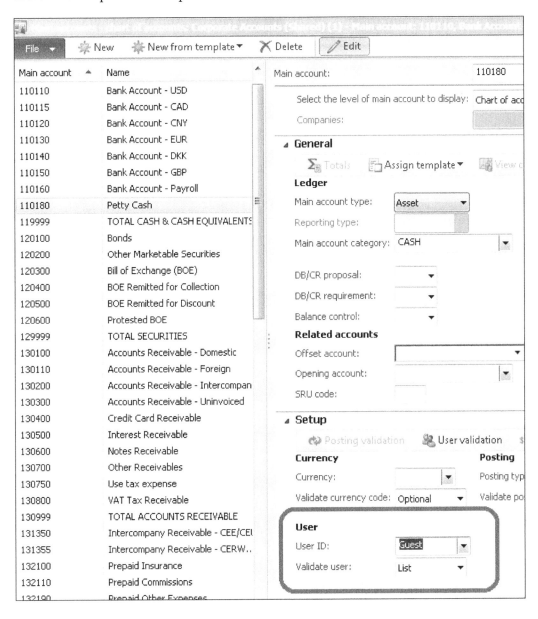

User validation is only activated if the selected validation is a list.

During the processing of a transaction; if an unauthorized accountant tries to post a transaction on the main account, an **Infolog** will pop up: **You are not authorized to use account #####**, as shown in the following screenshot:

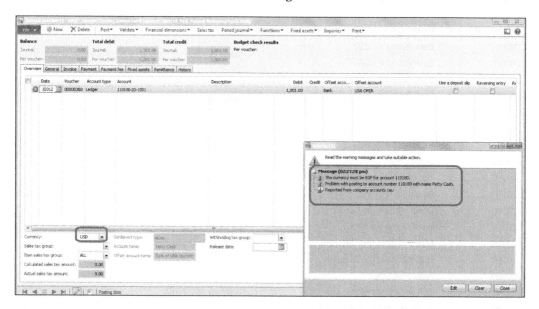

Posting type

Posting type validation is a control that is used to stop posting on a specific type of transaction of the main account.

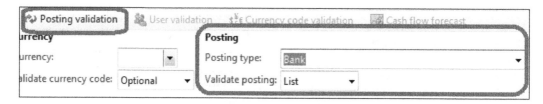

During the processing of a transaction; if a transaction breaks the posting type of the main account, an **Infolog** will pop up: **The posting type for account ##### is not valid**, as shown in the following screenshot:

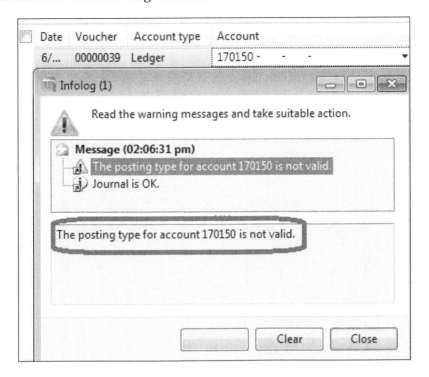

Understanding shared financial data

Microsoft Dynamics AX 2012 R2 introduced a new concept called shared financial data, which reduces the effort and time of deployment in a multiple-company environment and operational maintenance as well. The following diagram explains the concept of shared financial data in detail:

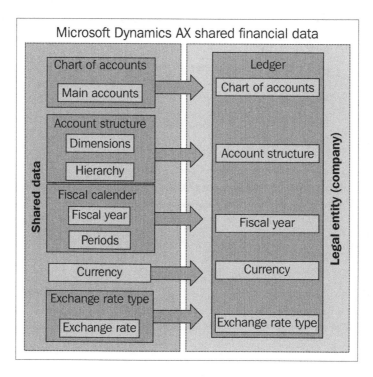

The financial data that will be shared between companies is as follows:

- **Chart of accounts**: This contains the main account
- **Account structure**: This contains the applicable dimensions of the main accounts
- **Fiscal year**: This contains the start date and end date of the fiscal year and the period's management
- **Currencies**: This represents the default currency and reporting currency
- **Exchange rate type**: This sets the monthly exchange rate for foreign currencies and the default budget exchange rate

To access the ledger window, navigate to **General ledger | Setup | Ledger**.
The following screenshot shows the Microsoft Dynamics AX 2012 R2 ledger:

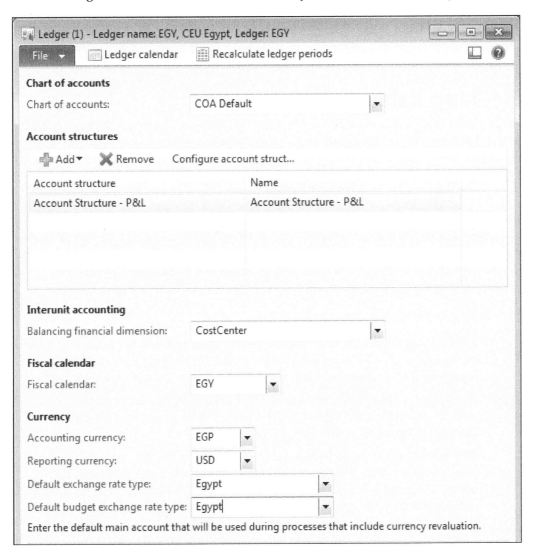

Understanding financial management in action

Here we will understand the process of financial management through the opening balance and various daily transactions.

Opening balance

When a company migrates from a legacy ERP solution to Microsoft Dynamics AX, one of the important data migration tasks is creating opening balances in the new Dynamics AX system based on the closing balances of the previous closed period (often the fiscal year) from the legacy system.

In order to ensure the accuracy of your Dynamics AX's opening balances, it is important to take a systematic approach to the process of planning, designing, and executing the migration of data for trial balances and subledgers, as well as validation and reconciliation of these elements along with general ledger, subledger, and financial dimensions. In this section, we will lay out the process and elements involved in creating new opening balances in Microsoft Dynamics AX from a legacy system.

The opening balances elements are as follows:

- **Trial balance report**: This consists of data about balance accounts that move their balances from one year to another, and profit and loss accounts that represent the income statement results and do not move to another year.

- **Subledger**: This consists of data about fixed assets, banks, vendors, customers, and items. Subledgers are linked to the chart of accounts through the posting profile setup.

- **Validation and reconciliation**: This validates that the balance of subledgers (fixed assets, banks, vendors, customers, and items) must represent the balance of general ledger accounts (trial balance) with respect to the financial dimensions balance (business units, department, and purpose), in case it is used through submodules. The controllership and financial consultants should finalize and validate the design and deployment of financial dimensions or dimension rules

Data integrity between the general ledger, subledger, and financial dimension is one of the main objectives of ERP. It must be considered from day one of the opening balances, as the opening balance transactions may affect daily transactions after going live.

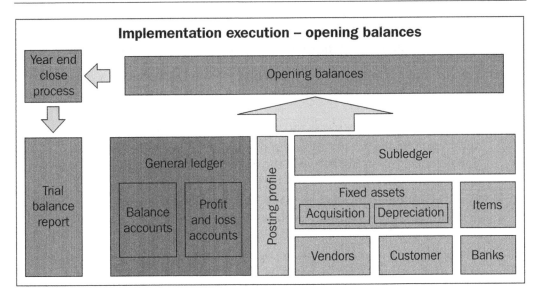

Opening balance best practices

After various attempts to upload opening balances to Microsoft Dynamics AX, the commonly followed approach is to separate the upload of ledger accounts (trial balance) and subledgers (vendors, customers, bank, inventory, and fixed assets). This is by using an error account in the subledger entries as debit and credit sides only in order to balance the subledger.

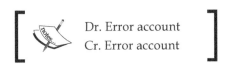

Dr. Error account
Cr. Error account

This approach took much time and effort in order to ensure that the general ledger's accounts and subledgers are reconciled, as well as to ensure the balance of error account is zero. Also, the opening balance methodology must be aligned with the financial controller.

Planning and designing

The following steps should be followed in the planning and designing phase:

- Prepare and upload the master data into Microsoft Dynamics AX (chart of accounts, banks, fixed assets, financial dimensions, vendors, customers, and inventory items).

- Maintain a high level of coordination between the controllership and application financial consultants in the design phase, including the finalization of mapping between the old chart of accounts (legacy system) and the new one.

- The application financial consultants should ensure the setup of the required fields in the data-collection template that he/she will use in order to upload the opening balance.

- The accountant who will fill in the opening balance data collection sheet must understand the fields and how he/she will fill them in.

- Create a separate journal name under the general ledger journal and voucher number sequence for easier tracking.

- Create separate journal names under **Inventory Management** (the movement journal) and voucher number sequence for easier tracking.

- If adjustments are needed for the opening balance, use the same journal name and voucher.

- The opening balances of general ledger and subledger are uploaded together. Avoid separating the general ledger's upload and the subledger's upload as far as you can.

- The subledger's (vendors and customers) posting profiles should be assigned to the opening balance.

Execution

The opening balance will be executed in three waves: the acquistion of fixed assets and depreciation, items, and trial balance with subledger. Here are the methods we utilize to ensure correct execution:

- Wave one: Fixed assets. The following are the methods to be used:
  - Fixed assets acquisition will be executed through a fixed assets acquisition proposal. The posting profile setup will generate the following entry:

 Dr. Fixed assets Acquisition Accounts (Balance)
Cr. Error Account.

If there are fixed assets that are acquired in a foreign currency, modify the acquisition entry with the currency's exchange rate.

- Fixed assets depreciation will be executed through a fixed assets depreciation proposal. The posting profile setup will generate the following entry:

> Dr. Error Account
> Cr. Accumulated Depreciation Accounts

- Wave two: Inventory items. The following is the method:
  - The inventory opening balance will be uploaded from the movement journal (the inventory subledger). The posting profile setup will generate the following entry:

> Dr. Inventory Accounts (Balance)
> Cr. Error Account

- Wave three: Trial balance with subledger. The following are the methods:
  - Identify the GL account balances that are not affected by the subledger's posting profiles
  - General ledger accounts that are affected by subledgers will be broken down by their relevant subledgers (banks, vendors, and customers) and the accounts will be affected directly by the subledger's posting profile
  - Make sure the assigned posting profile is the proper posting profile for each customer/vendor; this is for two reasons:

> First, make sure the customers/vendors' opening balance hits the right account, whether it is an advances account or general payable/receivable account.
> Second, ensure that the entries occurred during the settlement process (during the year's operations)

  - Replace the fixed assets accounts with an error account in order to close the amount in the error account, which resulted from acquisition transactions

    °   Replace the depreciation account with an error account in order to close the amount in the error account, which resulted from depreciation transactions

    °   If there are balances in a foreign currency, upload the opening balance entry with the currency's exchange rate

Validation

Validation performs the following tasks:

- Closing voucher to transfer all profit and loss balances to the retained earnings account
- Prints the trial balance report with the closing balance criteria

Performing daily transactions

The performance daily transactions section covers the functionalities that help the end users' daily work, which facilitates the entry process and thereby saves time and effort.

As seen in the following figure, there are three main functionalities, **Account Alias** (which is a new functionality delivered in Microsoft Dynamics AX 2012), **Recurring Entries**, and **Save Voucher**:

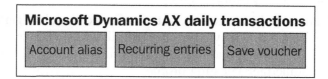

The account alias

The main account alias is a function that can be utilized for non-financial users who are not aware of the structure of a chart of accounts and the requirements to input data for a financial transaction. The main account aliases give the option to enter a predefined code for every combination of main accounts along with the financial dimensions. It is an alternative manually selecting an individual dimension combination for every transaction. This is a usability function.

To access the account alias window, navigate to **General ledger | Setup | Chart of accounts | Ledger account alias**.

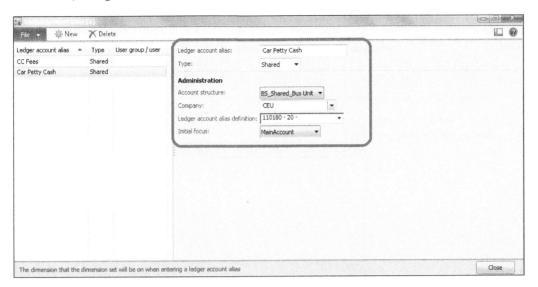

In the **Account** column, enter the defined main account alias and click on the combobox; it filters to the entered alias and shows the account's structure as well.

Then select the alias description and it is populated in the **Account** column with the account structure combination. The mouse cursor will be on a segment that has been specified in the **Initial focus** field in the setup form.

To access the general journal window, navigate to **General ledger | Journals | General journal | Lines**.

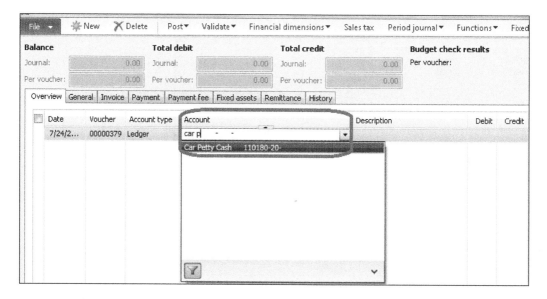

Recurring entries

Recurring entries are generally used for frequent transaction entries such as rentals and subscriptions. The accountant is able to create a periodic journal and generate an entry based on the transaction periods that are already set up.

Saving a voucher

Save a posted voucher and retrieve it in a new voucher. This is generally used for a long transaction entry.

Select a posted transaction to be saved. The options for saving are in percentages or an amount.

To access the save voucher window, navigate to **General ledger | Journals | General journal | Posted | Lines | Functions | Save voucher template**, as shown in the following screenshot:

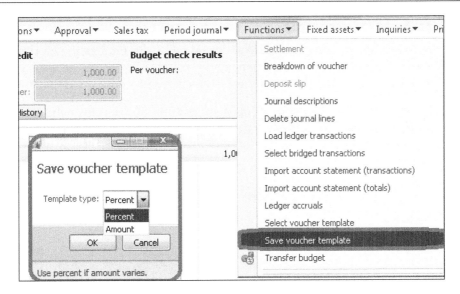

In order to create a new voucher, click on **Functions** and then click on **Select voucher template**, as shown in the following screenshot:

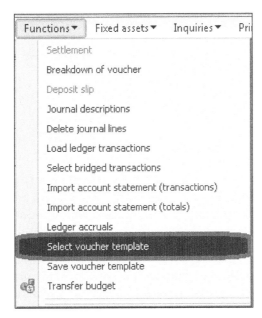

Microsoft Dynamics AX will show all the saved vouchers in headers and lines, displaying both sides of the transaction. A particular voucher will create a new "un-posted" voucher.

Closing procedure

Closing procedure is a common practice at organizations to finalize the monthly transactions and report the monthly financial reporting. The procedure varies from one company to another, but it has common steps between company departments.

The finance controllership department has responsibility for the closing procedure, where accountants follow up with the operations department to confirm they have posted the monthly transactions in the ERP. The following figure explains the closing procedure in detail:

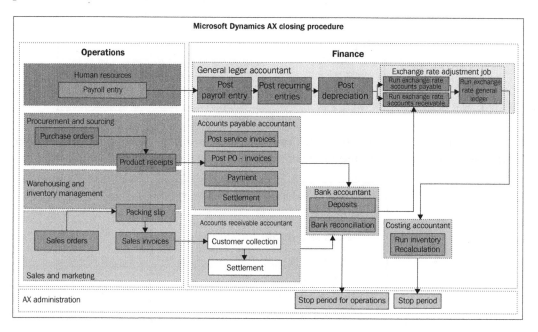

All the departments in a company are involved in the monthly closing process. The **Human resources** department calculates the payroll and generates the payroll entry to be validated and posted by the general ledger's accountant.

The **Procurement** department ensures they have confirmed all purchase orders to be received at the warehouse and the warehouse keeper confirms receiving them as it affects the inventory quantities and values. On the other side, the accounts payable accountants match and post purchase order invoices as well as service invoices. They then execute payments of due invoices that are related to the closing month.

The **Sales** department verifies that they have confirmed all sales orders to be delivered to the customer and issues sales invoices accordingly, which generates the revenue and cost of goods sold. In the **Finance** department, the accounts receivable accountant posts the customers' collections and settlements.

At that time, the fiscal period is stopped for all operations to prevent any further operational entries in that month and only the financial team is allowed to post the financial adjustment entries.

The general ledger's accountant posts the recurring entries, such as rental and accruals. So first run the fixed assets depreciation and exchange rate adjustment for subledgers (accounts payable and accounts receivable) and then run the exchange rate adjustments for the general ledger.

The costing accountant runs the inventory recalculation to adjust the average cost of inventory items and adjusts the sold quantities by the proper cost. He/she stops the fiscal period after finalizing the inventory calculation.

The management of financial periods is an administrative task. There are three stages for the period status.

To access the period status window, navigate to **General ledger | Setup | Ledger | Ledger calendar | Periods**.

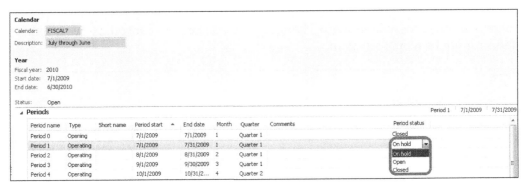

All transactions that are executed have the **Open** status in the **Period status** drop-down list.

After ensuring that all departments have entered and posted their transactions (relevant to the current month) as well as the financial post (the month-end adjustment transactions), the financial period status drop-down list is set to open for a specific user group and modules.

In order to access the modules' access-level path, navigate to **General ledger | Setup | Ledger | Ledger calendar | Modules access level**.

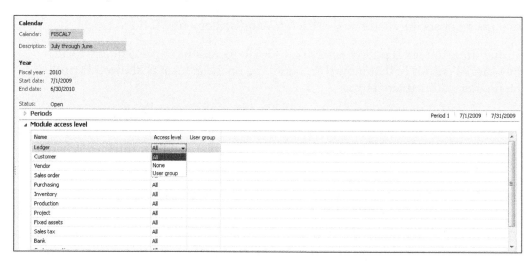

After dealing with the details of the financial department, make all the required adjustments for the current month. The financial **Period status** drop-down list is set to **On Hold** (formerly known as **Stopped** in Microsoft Dynamics AX 2009), which prevents any entry being posted in that period; but it can be reopened after that.

There is another possible scenario: changing **Period status** to **Closed**. However, this status cannot be reopened again.

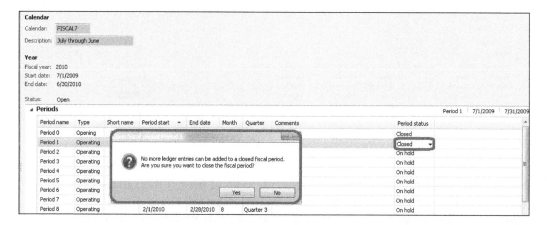

Summary

In this chapter, we discussed the practices in the financial implementations of Microsoft Dynamics AX 2012. We focused on the general ledger, covering the types of main accounts, classifications, and control points. We also explained shared financial data, which is a new function introduced in Microsoft Dynamics AX 2012 R2. We also learned about opening balance best practices, daily transactions, and the monthly closing procedure.

In the next chapter, we will cover bank management basic configurations, controls, and integrations with other modules (general ledger, accounts payable, and accounts receivable), and will also perform a bank reconciliation.

Summary

2
Understanding Cash and Bank Management

The cash and bank module is the place where a company's bank account, current and deposit accounts are listed. This chapter covers the following topics:

- Understanding cash and bank integration
- Controlling cash and bank management
- Exploring cash and bank management in action
- Bank account reconciliation

Understanding cash and bank integration

The modules' transactions represent the customer's deposits in the company's bank accounts, either by cash or by cheque, and also payments to vendors through cash/cheque. Bank reconciliation is an important procedure performed weekly or monthly (according to the number of transactions and the customers' business needs). This process should be performed once a month before the closing period to ensure that bank transactions (bank statements) are matched with book transactions, which are recorded in Microsoft Dynamics AX.

The following diagram shows the integration of cash and bank management:

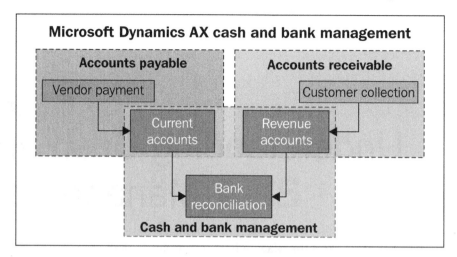

The cash and bank module is a shared module between the **Accounts payable** module and the **Accounts receivable** module (as seen in the previous diagram), where the vendors' payments are executed by a cheque or cash that can be printed through Microsoft Dynamics AX. The customers' collections are deposited into the bank's account. The key factor here is the method of payment, which is assigned to a transaction level that may recall a specific bank account ID, require a cheque number, fire payment steps for the cheque process, and so on.

Controlling cash and bank management

Microsoft Dynamics AX offers five main controls over bank and cash management. It is one of the key objectives of ERP that it controls in order to make the most of values of having an ERP application in place. These control functionalities should be highlighted to the process owners to be utilized efficiently.

Microsoft Dynamics AX 2012 emphasizes control as well as new business functionalities. Some of these controls were newly introduced in Microsoft Dynamics AX 2012. Some of the major controls in the cash and bank management module are shown in the following diagram:

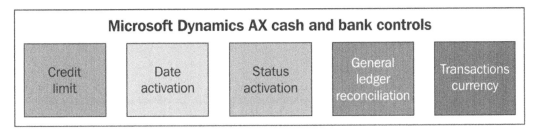

These Microsoft Dynamics AX cash and bank controls are explained in detail as follows:

- **Credit limit**: This allows for credit limit control on the bank account. This is a new feature introduced in the cash and bank management module.

- **Date activation**: This detects activation dates control. This is also a new feature in the cash and bank management module.

- **Status activation**: This detects the activation status on bank transactions. It's a new feature added in the cash and bank management module.

- **General ledger reconciliation**: This assigns one ledger account to more than one bank account.

- **Transaction currency**: This allows multiple currency transactions to be executed on the bank account.

Credit limit

The credit limit control stops posting transactions if it exceeds the credit limit that the bank can propose. To access cash and bank credit limit tolerance window, navigate to **Cash and bank management | Setup | Cash and bank management parameters | General**. The following screenshot explains the credit limit tolerance control:

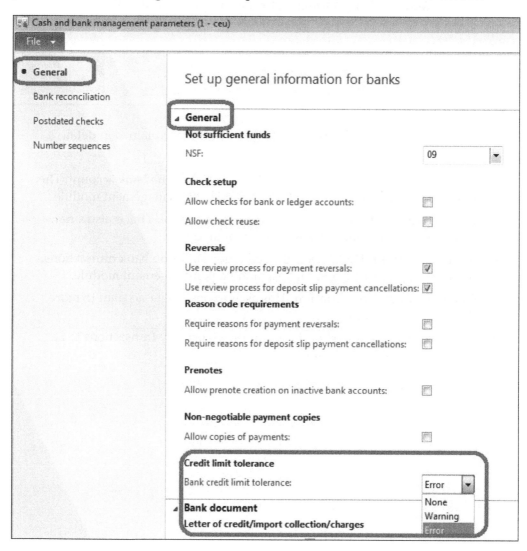

The **Credit limit tolerance** field must be activated under **Cash and bank parameters**, where it gives a warning or an error, or it is deactivated. The credit limit amount is defined for every bank account under general information. The amount must be negative; if it is not, you will receive this message: **Credit limit must be in negative**, as you can see in the following screenshot. For cash and bank credit limit tolerance, navigate to **Cash and bank management | Common | Bank accounts**.

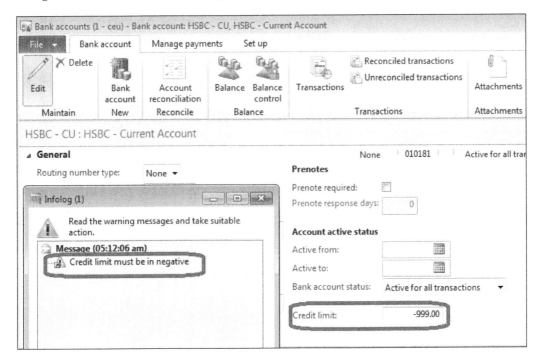

In the course of transaction processing, if an accountant validates or posts a credited amount that surpasses the bank's credit limit, an **Infolog** will **pop up**: **You cannot post the journal because the bank's credit limit has been exceeded**, as shown in the following screenshot:

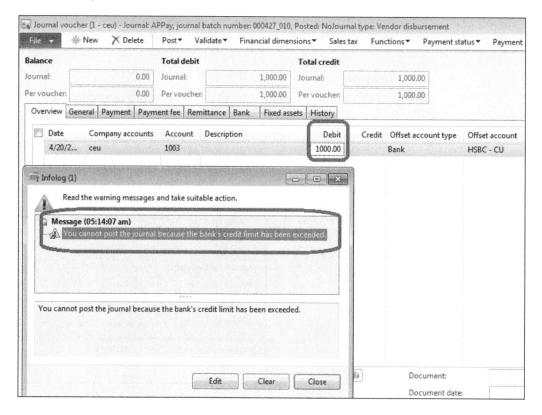

Date activation

Date activation of the bank account recognizes the activation range for every bank account. To access cash and bank date activation window, navigate to **Cash and bank management | Common | Bank accounts**.

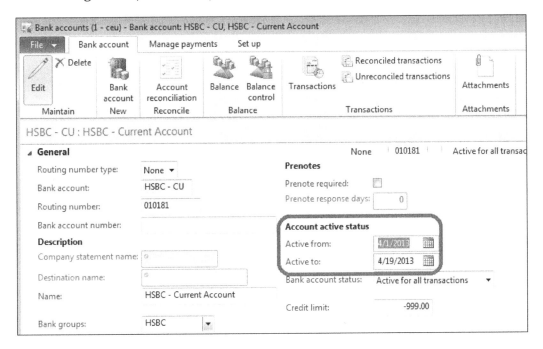

In the course of transaction processing, if an accountant posts or validates a transaction date which is not in the active date range, an infolog will pop up: **You cannot use the company bank account 'HSBC – CU' for this transaction because that bank account is not active**, as you can see in the following screenshot:

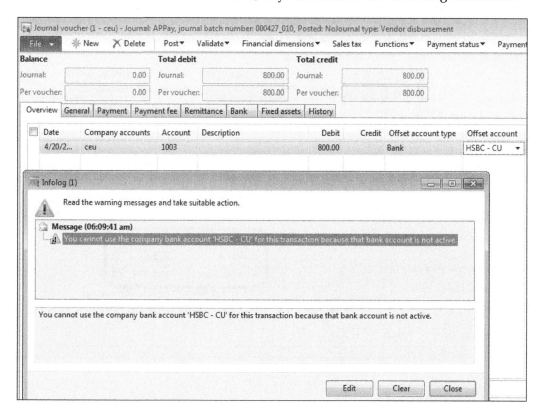

Status activation

As you can see in the following screenshot, status activation has three options: **Active for all transactions, Inactive for new transactions**, and **Inactive for all transactions**. To access cash and bank status activation window, navigate to **Cash and bank management | Common | Bank accounts**.

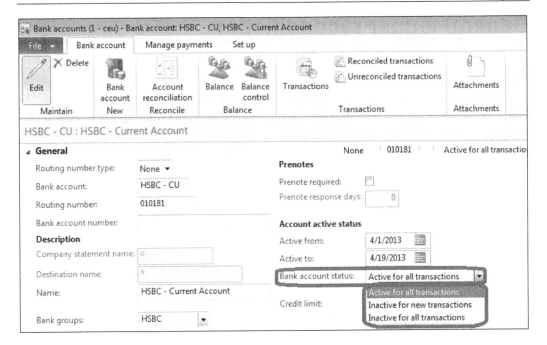

The three options of status activation are explained in detail as follows:

- **Active for all transactions**: This means a bank account is active and available for all transactions.

- **Inactive for new transactions**: This means no new transactions can be posted for a bank account. The existing transactions that have not yet been finalized, such as pending payments, will still take place as they were originally posted.

- **Inactive for all transactions**: This means no transactions, either new or existing, can be processed for a bank account.

General ledger reconciliation

The creation process of a new bank account must be assigned to a main account. Microsoft Dynamics AX 2012 gives a warning message to say that this account is already assigned to another bank's main account, and that should be considered during the reconciliation process with general ledger's main accounts. As seen in the following screenshot, the warning message that appears is: **Main account ##### is already used by bank account USA OPER. If you associate multiple bank accounts with a main account, the General Ledger Bank Reconciliation report will contain information from multiple bank accounts**:

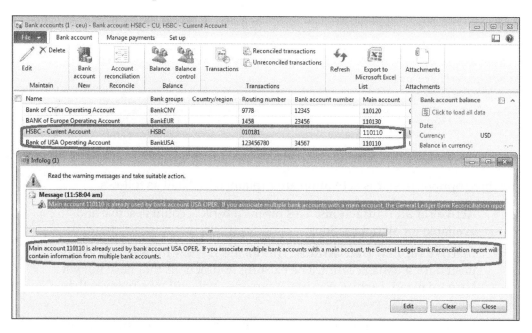

Transaction currency

The transaction currency for bank accounts could be one currency or multiple currencies; it is suggested to assign a single currency for every bank account. In the course of transaction processing, if an accountant tries to post an entry in a bank account that does not permit multiple currencies, an **Infolog** will pop up: **Currency EUR not allowed for account HSBC - CU**, as shown in the following screenshot:

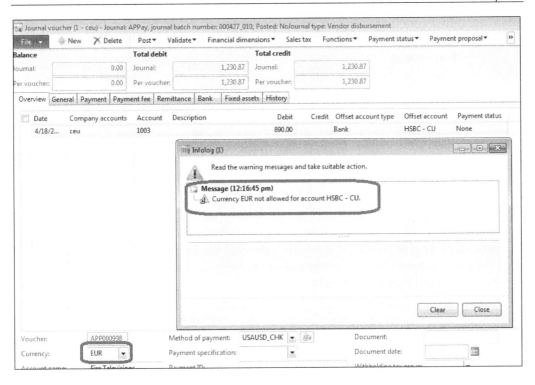

Exploring cash and bank management in action

The following section will explore cash and bank management in daily transaction. It will focus on bank account reconciliation, which is a key process to ensure that all recorded transactions match the bank statement.

Bank account reconciliation

Bank account reconciliation is a validation process of the bank's account statement and recorded transactions in the cash and bank management module through customer deposits and vendor payments.

There are two reconciliation mechanisms that you can apply for each bank account: the first one is the manual reconciliation mechanism and the second one is newly introduced in Microsoft Dynamics AX 2012 R2, the automatic import of bank statements.

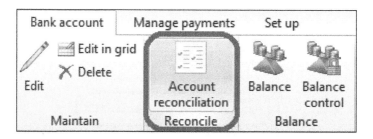

The procedure begins when the company receives the bank account statement from the bank. Under **Account reconciliation**, enter reconciliation date, statement number, and statement ending balance.

Under reconciliation transactions, the booked transactions through Microsoft Dynamics AX modules are listed. If it matches the bank statement, mark it as **Cleared**, as you can see in the following screenshot:

After marking all transactions, click on **Reconcile account** to confirm the reconciliation process. If the reconciliation is successful, an **Infolog** message is displayed on the screen: **Account has been reconciled**, as seen in the following screenshot:

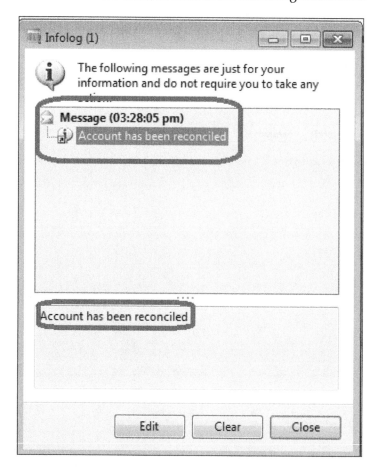

To automatically import bank statements, you must activate the **Advanced bank reconciliation** option. In order to activate the advanced bank reconciliation option, navigate to **Cash and bank management | Common | Bank accounts | Edit | Reconciliation**. The following screenshot displays the **Advanced bank reconciliation** option under **Reconciliation**:

As you can see in the following screenshot, the advanced bank reconciliation option cannot be turned off after activation:

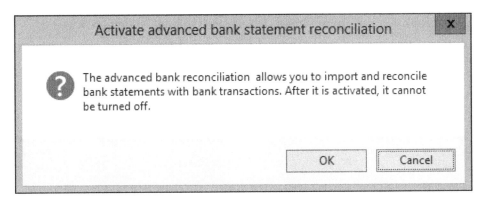

The following screenshot shows the generate bank documents screen:

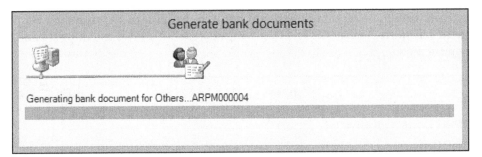

The process of importing bank statements starts by selecting **Bank account** and then by clicking on **Bank statements**, as you can see in the following screenshot. In order to go to the bank statement section, navigate to **Cash and bank management | Common | Bank accounts | Bank statement**.

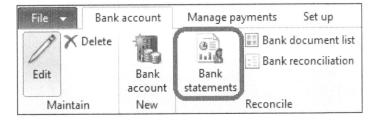

In the bank statement form, a line has been created with a status of **Open**. To import the bank statement, click on **Import statement**. To go to the bank statement section, navigate to **Cash and bank management | Common | Bank statement**. The following screenshot shows the bank statement screen:

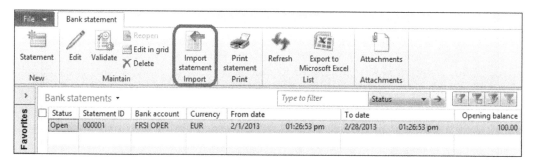

A dialog box will pop up to select the file to be imported. Choose a bank account, locate the file path, and then click on **OK**. In order to go to import bank statement section, you have to navigate to **Cash and bank management | Common | Bank statement | Import statement**. The following screenshot shows the import bank statement screen:

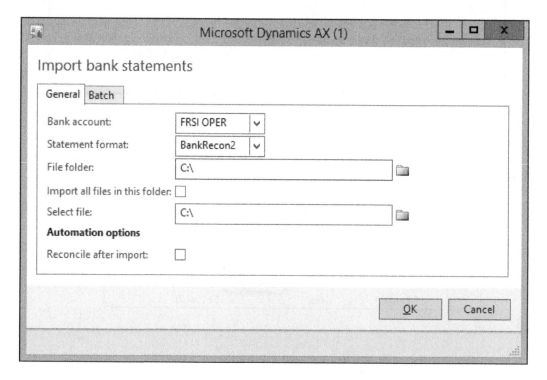

The bank statement form contains the transaction lines of the imported bank transactions, in addition to the opening balance, ending balance, and net amount details. Click on **Validate** to validate the imported bank statement. If there is an error with the opening or ending balance, the validation process will stop. In order to edit the bank statement, you have to navigate to **Cash and bank management | Common | Bank statement | Edit**. The following screenshot shows the bank statement screen:

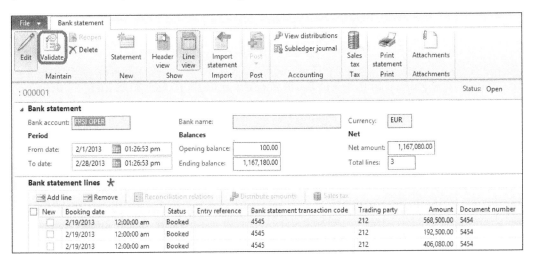

As you can see in the following screenshot, an **Infolog** message will pop up to confirm that the statement passes the validation process:

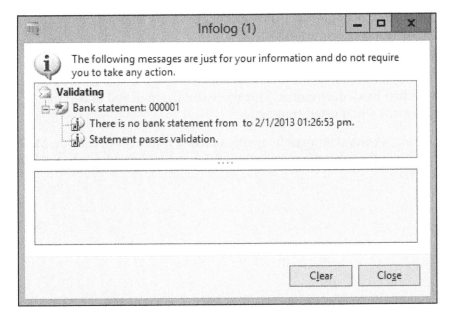

In order to match the bank transactions with the bank statement, go to the bank reconciliation journal. For bank reconciliation journal, navigate to **Cash and bank management | Journals | Bank reconciliation**, as shown in the following screenshot:

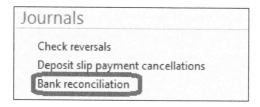

To create a new journal line, select **Bank account** and then click on **Lines**, as shown in the following screenshot:

The bank reconciliation worksheet contains the following fields:

- **Open statement lines**: This represent the imported transactions of the bank statement
- **Open bank documents**: This represent the bank transactions posted on Microsoft Dynamics AX
- **Matched statement lines**: This represent the matched line in the statement with posted transactions
- **Matched bank documents**: This represent the matched line in the statement with posted transactions

While checking a bank statement line with a posted transaction, click on **Match**. As you can see in the following screenshot, the matched lines move to the **Matched documents** tab:

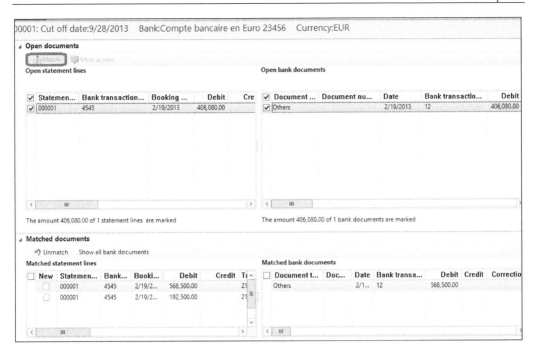

After matching all transactions against the bank statement, click on **Reconcile** (as shown in the following screenshot) in order to reconcile this statement and close it:

As you can see in the following screenshot, an **Infolog** will pop up indicating that the reconciliation process is finished:

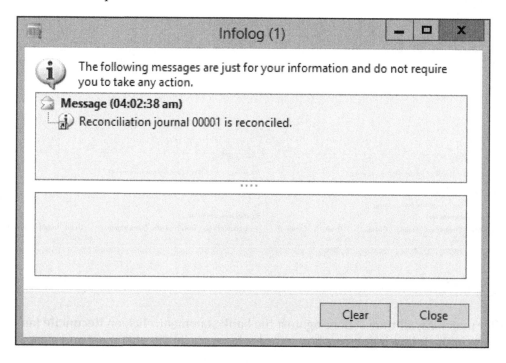

Summary

This chapter covers the integration of the cash and bank modules with accounts payable, accounts receivable, and general ledger. We discussed the controls offered by Microsoft Dynamics AX 2012. We also explored the bank reconciliation transactions that are executed at the end of each month.

In the next chapter, we will discuss the cash flow management integration concept, basic configurations, and transactions.

Functioning of Cash Flow Management

3

Cash flow management is a tool that predicts a company's future cash needs in the future. Cash flow management mainly covers the cash out and cash in events. Cash out is generated from the company's expenditure against the goods/services purchased, whereas cash in is generated from the company's revenue against the sale of goods/services. It gives the company's management a vision of the cash position in order to efficiently manage vendor payments in a specific period, and also the customer collections during the same period, to protect the company's cash situation. This chapter will cover the following topics:

- Understanding cash flow integration with other modules
- Exploring cash flow forecast configuration
- Working with cash flow transactions
- Forecasting cash flow by currency requirements
- Forecasting the main account's cash flow

Understanding cash flow integration with other modules

The integrated modules of cash flow management are **Accounts payable**, **Accounts receivable**, and **General ledger**. The accounts payable module manages the vendor payments process, the accounts receivable module manages the customer collections process, and the general ledger module identifies the cash and cash equivalent accounts. The following figure shows the integration of the cash flow modules:

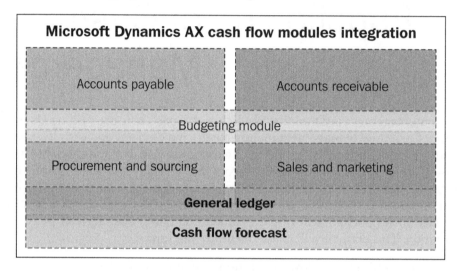

The modules that are integrated in cash flow forecast management are divided into the following groups:

- Vendor expenditure management has the following elements:
    - **Accounts payable**: This identifies the vendors' terms of payment, settlement periods, vendors' posting profiles, accounts used for vendor settlement, and vendor invoice transaction execution
    - **Procurement and sourcing**: This identifies the transactional execution of vendor purchase orders and receptions

- Customer collections management:
    - **Accounts receivable**: This identifies the customers' terms of payment, settlement periods, customer posting profiles, accounts used for customer settlement, and customer invoice transaction execution
    - **Sales and marketing**: This identifies the transactional execution of customer sales orders, issuances, and invoicing

- **Budgeting**: This identifies the budget distributions based on specific time intervals (years, months, and days)
- **General ledger**: This identifies the cash and cash equivalent accounts that represent the liquidity account
- **Cash flow forecast**: This represents the cash flow position for purchase and sales order transactions

With the Microsoft Dynamics AX consultant, the implementation of cash flow forecast management is a mutual effort between the controller, accounting manager, treasury, budgeting, procurement, and sales.

Cash flow forecast configuration

The cash flow forecast configuration and setups are combined with the integrated modules of cash flow management. The following figure explains the cash flow forecast configuration in detail:

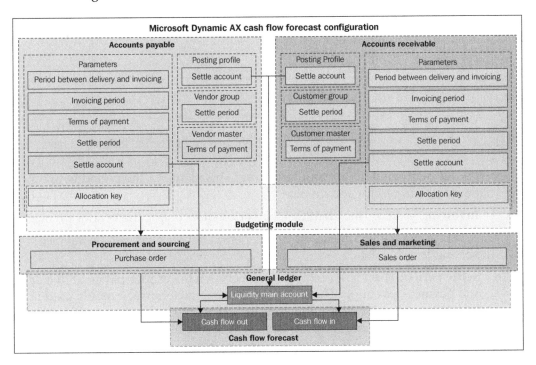

The main configuration and setup of cash flow forecast in Microsoft Dynamics AX is performed in the following modules:

Accounts payable

The accounts payable is again subdivided as follows:

- **Parameters**: This identifies the company-wide parameters for accounts payable. For accounts payable parameters, navigate to **Accounts payable | Setup | Accounts payable parameters | Ledger and sales tax | Cash flow forecast** as shown in the following screenshot:

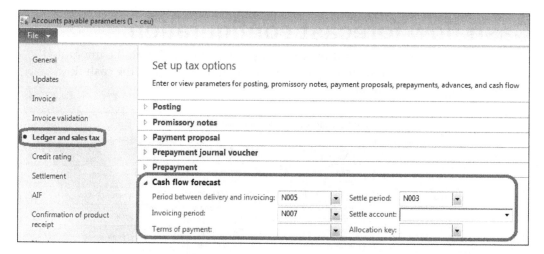

- **Period between delivery and invoicing**: This identifies the period between the products' receipt and invoice.

- **Invoicing period**: This identifies the period of receiving the vendor invoice.

- **Terms of payment**: This identifies the period between the vendor invoice posting and due date.

- **Settle period**: This identifies the period between the vendor payment due date and payment execution. The terms of payment values are commonly used in the accounts payable's cash flow forecast where we can set the number of days or months that identify the payment due date. For the accounts payable's terms of payment, navigate to **Accounts payable | Setup | Payment | Terms of payment**, as seen in the following screenshot:

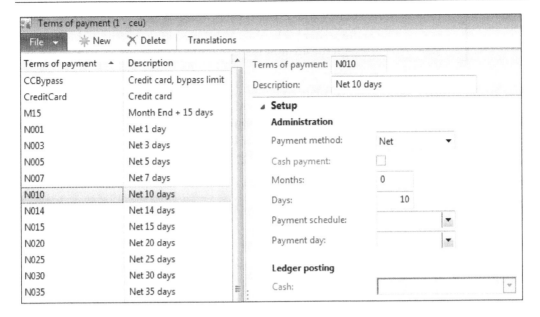

- **Vendor posting profiles**: This is an integration point between accounts payable and general ledger where identifying a particular ledger account will be used while posting a transaction for a specific vendor. The **Settle account** column in the following screenshot represents the liquidity accounts that are used for vendor payments. For the accounts payable posting profiles, navigate to **Accounts payable | Setup | Vendor posting profiles**. The following screenshot displays the vendor posting profiles page in detail:

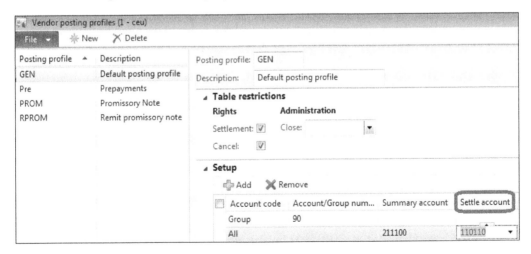

The **Settle account** column in **Vendor posting profile** overrides **Settle account** under module parameters.

- **Vendor groups**: This represents the vendor's classification and the posting profile assigned to a specific vendor group in order to identify the **Settle period** column that is used in cash flow management logic. For the accounts payable vendor groups profile, navigate to **Accounts Payable | Setup | Vendor | Vendor groups**. The following screenshot shows the **Vendor groups** screen:

Vendor group ▲	Description	Terms of payment	Settle period
10	Video Vendors	N030	
20	Audio Vendors	N030	N007 ▼
30	Services Vendors	N010	N001

Vendor groups (1 - ceu) - Vendor group: 20, Audio Vendors
File ▼ ✳ New ✕ Delete Record Item posting Default account setup Forecast

The **Settle period** column in **Vendor groups** overrides the **Settle period** column under module parameters.

- **Vendor master**: In the vendor master data information—which is captured and recorded during the creation of vendors and has an effect on vendor aging and cash flow forecast as well—the terms of payment under the payment section is considered as a default value, proposed when the vendor is selected in transaction and can be changed on a transactional level without modifying the master data record. For accounts payable vendor master data, navigate to **Accounts payable** | **Common** | **Vendors** | **All vendors**.

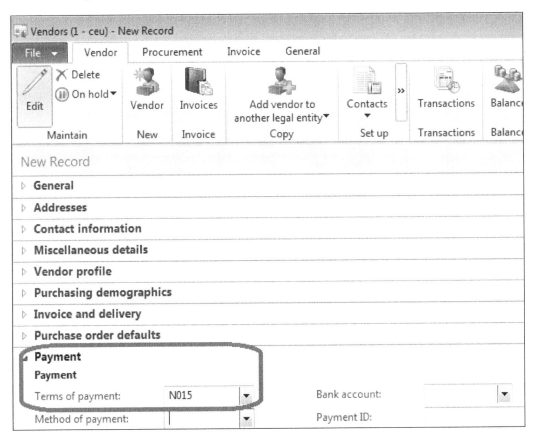

Accounts receivable

The accounts receivable module is subdivided as follows:

- **Parameters**: This identifies the company-wide parameters for accounts receivable. For accounts receivable parameters, navigate to **Accounts receivable | Setup | Accounts receivable parameters | Ledger and sales tax | Cash flow forecast**. The following screenshot shows **Ledger and sales tax** in detail:

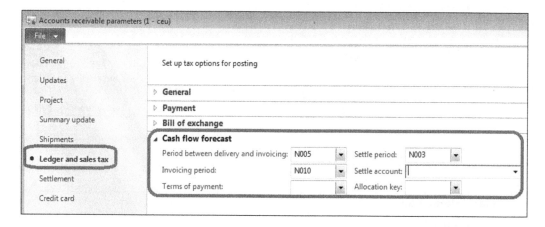

- **Period between delivery and invoicing**: This identifies the period between the products' issuance and invoicing.

- **Invoicing period**: This identifies the period of issuing the customer invoice.

- **Terms of payment**: This identifies the period between the customer invoice posting and due date.

- **Settle period**: This identifies the period between the customer payment due date and payment execution. The terms of payment values are commonly used in the accounts receivable's cash flow forecast, where we can set the number of days or months that identify the payment due date. For accounts receivable terms of payment, navigate to **Accounts receivable | Setup | Payment | Terms of payment** as shown in the following screenshot:

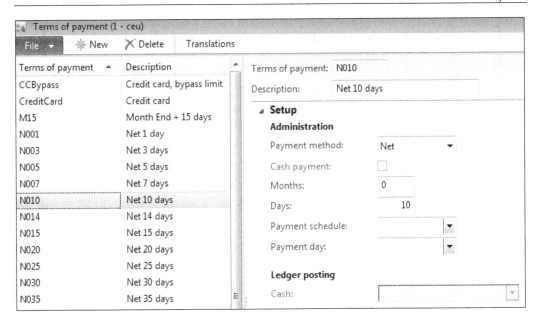

- **Customer posting profiles**: This is an integration point between accounts receivable and general ledger, where identifying the ledger account will be used when posting a transaction on a customer attached to a particular posting profile. The **Settle account** column in the following screenshot represents the liquidity accounts that are used for customer payments. For accounts receivable posting profiles, navigate to **Accounts receivable | Setup | Customer posting profiles**.

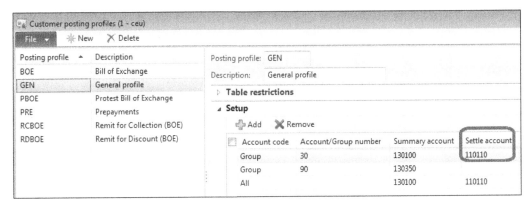

The **Settle account** column in **Customer posting profile** dominates the **Settle account** column under module parameters.

- **Customer groups**: This represents the customer classification and the posting profile assigned to a specific customer group. You can also see the **Settle period** column in the following screenshot, that is used in the cash flow management logic:

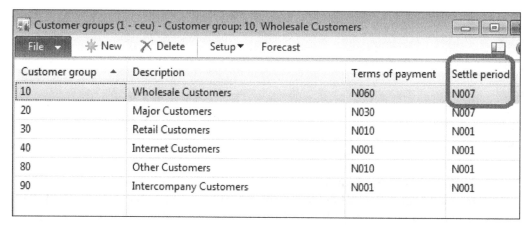

Microsoft Dynamics AX – customer groups under accounts receivable

 The **Settle period** column in **Customer groups** dominates the **Settle period** under module parameters.

- **Customer master**: In the customer master data information—which is captured and recorded during the creation of a customer and has an effect on customer aging and cash flow forecast as well—it is terms of payment under payment section in customer master data. It is considered as a default value proposed when the customer is selected in a transaction and could be changed on a transactional level without modifying the master data record.

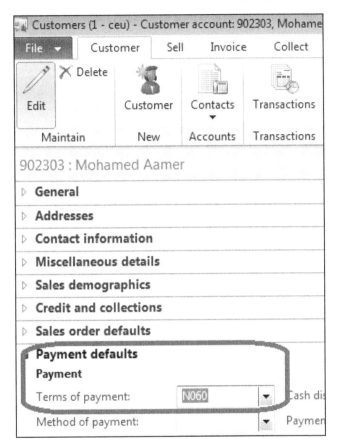

Budget

The core concepts in the budget module are as follows :

- **Allocation key**: This distributes the budgets for a specific period by a weight of allocation percentage, which could be day, month, and/or year. To access the budget allocation key window, navigate to **General ledger | Setup | Periods | Periods allocation categories**. Click on **Lines** to enter an allocation percentage for each period.

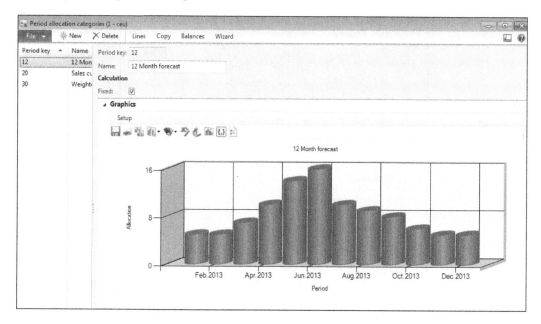

General ledger

The general ledger is subdivided as follows:

- **Main accounts**: The **Set up of cash flow forecasts** screen (as you can see in the following screenshot) represents the dependency of other accounts that will affect the company's cash flow. For example, sales tax payment. For the main account's cash flow, navigate to **General ledger | Setup | Chart of accounts | Chart of accounts**.
    - ○ Select **companies** in **Select the level of main account to display**

○ Click on **Cash flow forecast** as shown in the following screenshot:

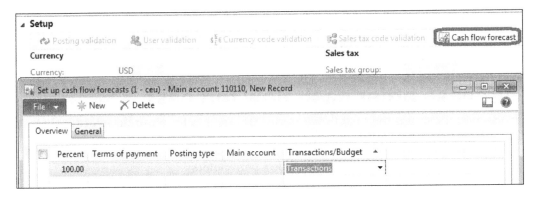

- **Liquidity accounts**: This lists the cash and cash equivalent accounts that are used to calculate the cash flow forecast:

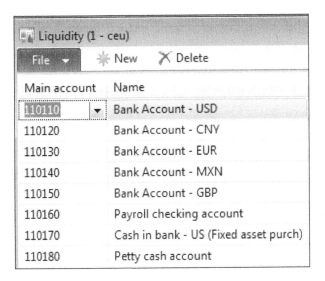

Cash flow transactions

The transactions that affect the cash flow forecast are purchase and sales orders. The cash flow transactions also depend on the configuration of the company-wide parameters and master data setup.

Purchase order cash flow forecast

This section illustrates the cash flow forecast transaction for a **purchase order (PO)**. The order data is as follows:

Configuration of accounts payable module's parameters:

Period between delivery and invoicing	5 days
Invoice period	7 days
Settle period	3 days

Vendor master data:

Terms of payment	**15 days**

Purchase order data:

Purchase order date	January 01, 2013
Purchase order Quantity	1 Pc
Currency	EGP
Default currency	USD
Exchange rate	1 USD = 5 EGP
Purchase price	5000 EGP = 1000 USD

The purchase order was created on January 01, 2013. Based on the setup of period between delivery and invoice, which is 5 days, the date will be January 6, 2013 (PO date + 5 days). Based on the setup of invoicing period, which is 7 days, the date will be January 13, 2013 (PO date + 5 days + 7 days). Based on the setup of terms of payment, which is 15 days, the date will be January 28, 2013 (PO date + 5 days + 7 days + 15 days). Based on the setup of settle period, which is 3 days, the date will be 31 January 2013 (PO date + 5 days + 7 days + 15 days +3 days). The following figure represents the cash flow forecast transaction in detail:

Microsoft Dynamics AX cash flow forecast				

Period between delivery and invoicing (5 days) | January 6, 2013

Invoicing period (7 days) | January 13, 2013

Terms of payment (15 days) | January 28, 2013

Settle period (3 days) | January 31, 2013

The **Cash flow forecasts** tab can be viewed under **Purchase order**. In the ribbon, navigate to the **Invoice** section, then go to the **Bill** group and select **cash flow forecasts** as shown in the following screenshot:

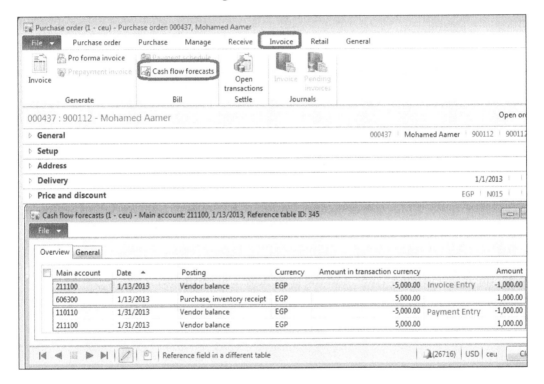

The invoice entry date is calculated based on the period between delivery and invoicing and invoice period (5 days + 7 days = January 13). The payment entry date is calculated based on the number of days in terms of payment, settle period, and the invoice date. (13 days + 15 days + 3 days = January 31).

Cash flow forecast by currency requirement

Microsoft Dynamics AX has a function which fulfills the currency requirement. This function is a currency requirement inquiry form. For cash flow forecast currency requirements, navigate to **General ledger** | **Periodic** | **Currency requirement** | **currency requirement**. The following screenshot shows the currency requirement screen:

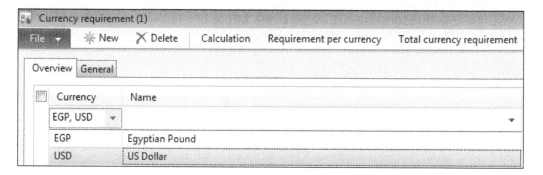

 In some cases, the cash flow forecast requirements are not calculated properly, thereby requiring you to run a cash flow forecast job. This job can be run manually or an automatic batch job can be set up.

The **Requirement per currency** tab represents the cash flow forecast for a specific currency code for a specific period. With reference to the previous transactions, select the **EGP** currency code, and the cash flow will be illustrated in a graph, as shown in the following screenshot:

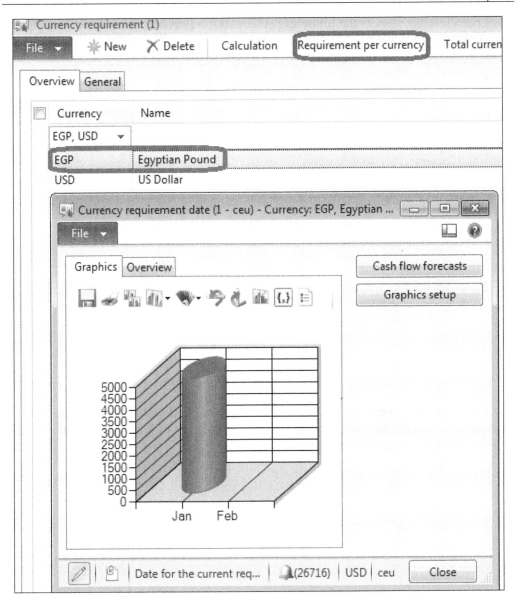

The **Overview** tab seen in the following screenshot represents the cash flow requirements per period:

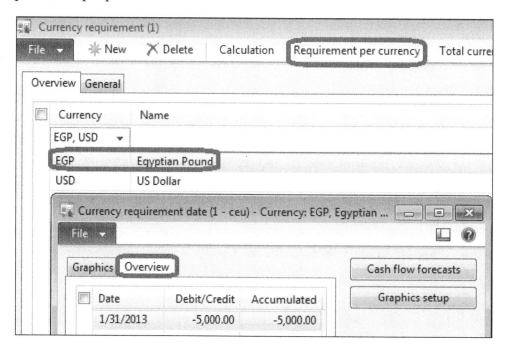

The **Total currency requirement** tab represents the cash flow forecast requirements by company, and the default currency is **USD**. This gives a clear vision for the projection of cash in and out for a specific period.

Main account cash flow forecast

The Main account, which has a setup for cash flow forecast, can view the cash flow of forecasts that are related to this main account.

Under the **General** tab, click on **View cash flow forecast** as you can see in the following screenshot:

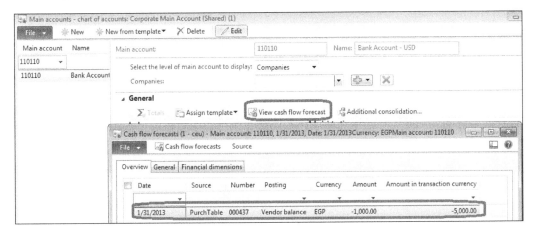

Summary

This chapter covers the basics of cash flow forecast configurations and setups in Microsoft Dynamics AX and the integration points between modules to facilitate cash flow function. We also showed a practical example of a cash flow transaction and inquiries, in addition to a forecast by currency and main account.

In the next chapter, we will discuss costing management from the inventory perspective as it is the most significant cost for an organization, and requires control and monitoring.

4
Working with Cost Management

The costing function is one of the most critical subjects in the ERP implementation, specifically inventory costing. This function requires intensive workshops during the implementation life cycle to contest the business costing model and how it will be mapped to Microsoft Dynamics AX.

In this chapter, we will cover the following topics:

- Understanding the business costing model
- Configuring inventory costing
- Exploring the inventory costing background (physical and financial update)
- Understanding inventory recalculation and closing
- Working with inventory marking

Understanding the business costing model

The highest significant cost of organizations is encumbered in the inventory costing. In that sense, one of the main objectives of ERP implementation is to manage, reduce, and control inventory costing. The inventory significantly affects the company's bottom line and profitability as well. The companies that carry inventory as a raw material for production bear the cost of inventory, which in turn affects the cost of production in addition to the goods in process and the **cost of goods sold** (**COGS**) accordingly. The companies that carry inventory as stock for sales bear the inventory cost, which in turn affects the cost of goods sold.

The main driver of inventory cost is the purchase cost from the vendor, in addition to all costs that are paid until the goods are received into the company's warehouse, such as freight, custom duties, and loading. All these are known as miscellaneous charges, which is a function name in AX.

The company's profitability is directly impacted by the inventory cost; therefore, it is essential for the organization to effectively manage the procurement activities and financial cost control that monitors inventory costs. The following figure shows Microsoft Dynamics AX inventory costing:

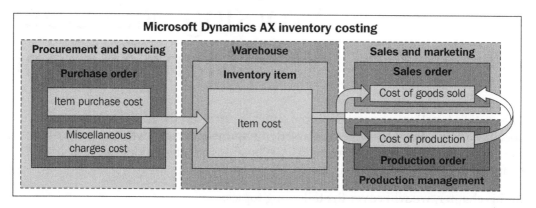

The implementation team ascertains the inventory costing strategy for the company. It is a joint effort between the financial controller, inventory and warehousing manager, and application consultant during the analysis phase of the implementation. The financial controller sets the inventory valuation method and inventory posting profiles. The inventory and warehousing manager sets the inventory item coding structure and item groups for inventory classifications. The application consultant maps the controller as well as the inventory and warehousing manager requirements to Microsoft Dynamics AX 2012.

Configuring inventory costing

The configuration and setup of inventory costing are combined between the integrated modules of inventory and warehousing management, product information management, and financial controls. A collective of all types of setup is shown in the product master form, depicted in the following figure:

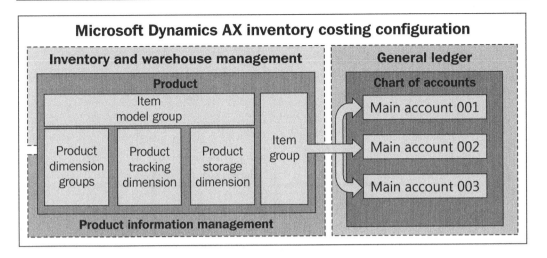

- **Item model group**: This identifies the inventory valuation method
- **Product dimension groups**: This identifies the product's attributes
- **Product storage dimension groups**: This identifies the product's location
- **Product tracking groups**: This identifies the product's tracking information

Item model group

The main configuration and setup of inventory costing in Microsoft Dynamics AX is in **Item model group,** where we identify the inventory costing valuation method. For inventory model group, navigate to **Inventory and warehouse management | Setup | Inventory | Item model group**. Microsoft Dynamics AX 2012 R2 supports the following inventory valuation methods:

- **FIFO**: This is first-in first-out
- **LIFO**: This is last-in first-out
- **LIFO date**: This is the last-in first-out date
- **Weighted avg.:** This is the weighted average
- **Weighted avg. date**: This is the weighted average date
- **Standard cost**: This is the standard cost
- **Moving average**: This is the moving average

The following screenshot shows all the inventory valuation methods:

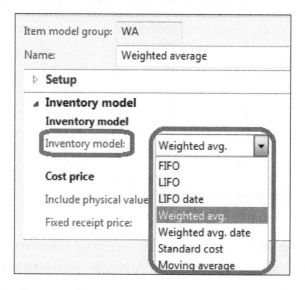

Product dimension groups

The following screenshot shows a product dimension group screen that represents the item attributes: **Configuration**, **Size**, **Color**, and **Style**:

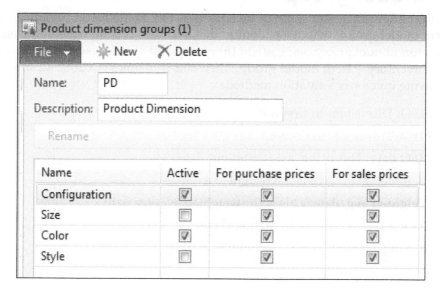

For product dimension groups, navigate to **Product information management** | **Setup** | **Dimension groups** | **Product dimension groups**.

Storage dimension groups

As you can see in the following screenshot, the **Storage dimension groups** screen sorts the required stock, keeping a note of the location, whether it is **Site**, **Warehouse**, **Location**, or **Pallet ID**. This assists in the reporting of inventory quantities and cost.

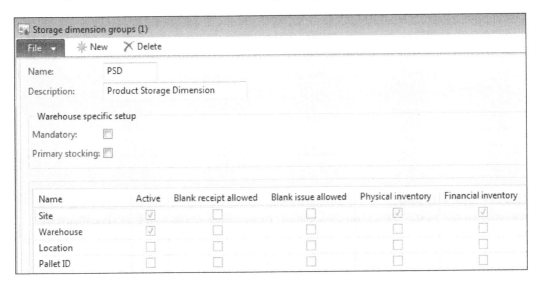

To access storage dimension window, navigate to **Product information management** | **Setup** | **Dimension groups** | **Storage dimension groups**.

Tracking dimension groups

The tracking dimension is a lower-level assortment of products, whether it is serial number for electronic inventory items or a batch number. For tracking dimension groups, navigate to **Product information management | Setup | Dimension groups | Tracking dimension groups**, as shown in the following screenshot:

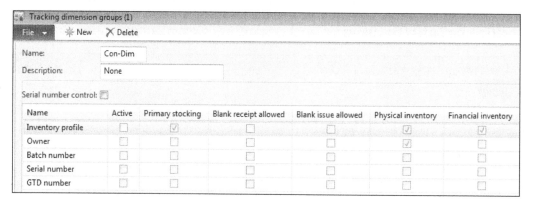

Item groups

As you can see in the following screenshot, **Item group** is the product classification for inventory items, and it is the integration point between the inventory and financial module. The classification of **Item groups** should be a joint effort between the stock management and the controller.

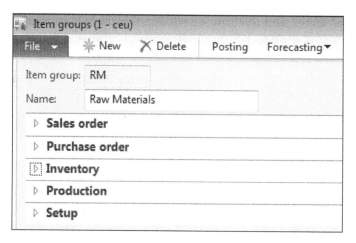

The inventory posting profile consists of the following possible inventory transactions:

- **Sales order**: This is a sales and marketing module transactions
- **Purchase order**: This is a procurement and sourcing module transactions
- **Inventory**: This is an inventory and warehousing management module transactions
- **Production**: This is production management module transactions

The posting profiles are the integration point between the subledgers and general ledger. It is a set of ledger accounts that are used to generate the automatic ledger entry in which a transaction occurs. It is possible to select different ledger accounts for each type of subledger transaction. Microsoft Dynamics AX offers flexibility in the setup of posting profiles. The posting could be on four different levels, as shown in the following figure:

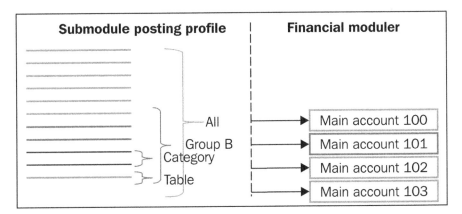

The posting domination levels are **All**, **Group**, **Category**, and **Table**. These are explained as follows:

- **Group B** dominates over **All**
- **Category** dominates over **Group B** and **All**
- **Table** dominates over **Category**, **Group**, and **All**

If the posting profile is for **All** and there are some groups that have been identified for a specific main account, then those will be excluded from the **All** setup. At the same time, if there is a category relation selected for a specific main account, then those categories will be excluded from the **All** and **Group** posting profiles. If there is a table relation selected for a specific main account, it will apply the **Table** posting profile. The following screenshot illustrates an example of all these posting domination levels:

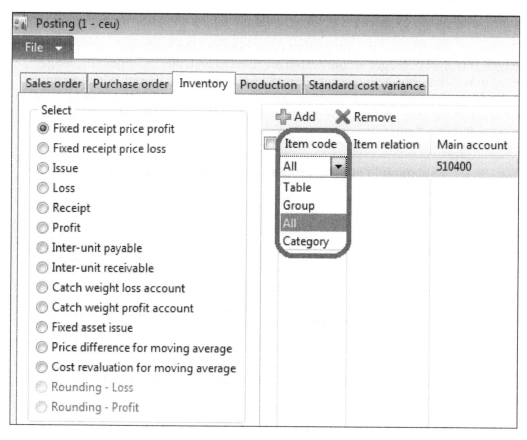

Exploring the inventory costing background

Highlighting the inventory costing model in Microsoft Dynamics AX in order to understand the inventory valuation methods, there are three main concepts: physical and financial update, inventory recalculation and closing, and marking.

Physical and financial updates

The physical and financial update considers real-life business scenarios where there is a difference between the reception costs and invoices. It works in uncertain business environments.

Physical update

The physical update represents the inventory transaction, whether it is a product receipt for purchase order or a packing slip for a sales order. The reception price inherits from the item purchase price in the purchase order and identifies the item cost price in the warehouse. The cost of goods sold is retrieved from the inventory cost price and the physical issuance occurred from the sales order. The following figure shows the physical and financial updates:

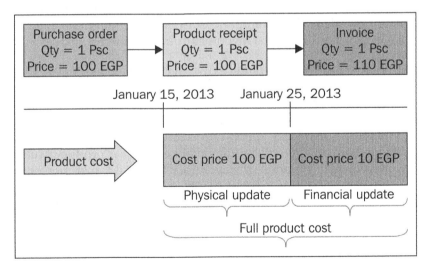

Financial update

The financial update represents the invoice posting, whether for a purchase order or a sales order. The sales order invoice only has an effect on sales revenue and cost of goods sold. While on the other hand, the purchase order invoice affects the inventory cost if there are changes in purchase price, be it an increase or decrease.

> If your business requires considering the miscellaneous charges in event of product reception, there is InventoryII solution offered by **Federation of Small Businesses (FSB)**.

The default mechanism of the financial update for purchase order in Microsoft Dynamics AX is that the financial update dominates the physical update in order to allocate the final item addition cost that will be reflected in the inventory. The physical update could be considered as an estimated cost, and the final cost is reflected in the purchase order invoice that will affect inventory cost in the warehouse sub module, and main account in the chart of accounts as well.

Understanding inventory recalculation and closing

The inventory recalculation is a normal procedure in the Microsoft Dynamics AX environment that calculates the inventory cost in the warehouse and adjusts the inventory issuances according to the inventory value model (the valuation method).

The inventory cost in Microsoft Dynamics AX is a running average cost. In order to apply the valuation method, the recalculation process should be run. The normal mechanism of the inventory cost calculation applies the inventory valuation method that is attached to the product master through running the recalculation function. The recalculation function mainly affects two areas: first, the item cost in the warehouse, and second, the inventory adjustment entries for product issuances from the inventory, which generates the inventory financial transaction entries.

> The inventory adjustment entries are generated when the issuance cost of the item is different from the current cost of the inventory items in the warehouse, according to the inventory model group (the valuation method). The entries are generated based on the original issuance transactions.
>
> For example: if the COGS of the sales order is 100 EGP and the current cost in the warehouse is 110 EGP, the recalculation process generates an entry by 10 EGP (Dr. COGS 10, Cr. Inventory 10).

The commonly applied valuation method is **Weighted Average Cost**, where the inventory issuances are valuated at the average cost of the items that are received during that period and also the on-hand inventory.

 Weight Average = (Received quantity * Received cost) + (On-hand quantity * On-hand cost) / (Received quantity + On-hand quantity).

The inventory cost is also considered as a tentative cost. The inventory issuances carry the current running average cost. The actual cost is applied after the recalculation process is done, and is based on the inventory valuation method that is configured in **Item model group**. The adjustment transactions represent the difference between the running average cost and the configured costing valuation method. To access the inventory close window, navigate to **Inventory and warehouse management | Periodic | Inventory close**. The following figure explains the inventory recalculation and closing concept:

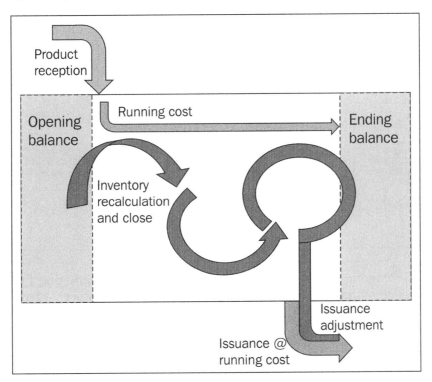

Working with inventory marking

During daily business in inventory management, there are some transactions that need to be returned to the inventory at the same cost at which they were issued. Each inventory transaction is associated to a unique Lot ID. Any inventory transaction is assigned to a Lot ID with an unique identification that helps in inventory cost and inventory transaction tracking; this is to specify the transaction's cost. The marking function can be used with **Sales order** to specify the cost of goods sold for the marked line in the **Sales order** lines, and it can be used in the issuance return (addition) from the movement journal, production order, and/or **bill of material (BOM)** journal.

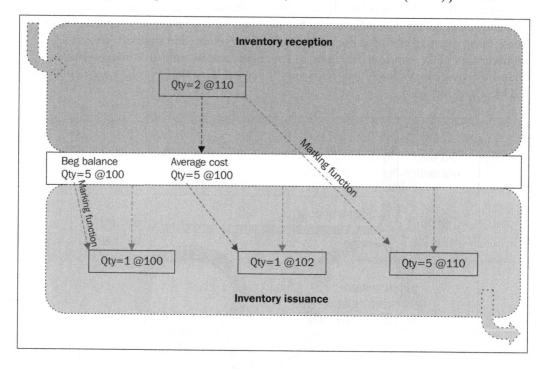

To access the marking function window, navigate to **Sales and marketing | Common | All sales orders | Sales order | Sales order lines form | Inventory | Marking**

Inventory management | Journals | Voucher lines | Inventory | Marking as you can see in the following screenshot:

As you can see in the following screenshot, the **Marking** form lists all the relevant transactions for the inventory item, which will be set to mark on. As you can see in the following screenshot, the **Set mark now** checkbox is checked:

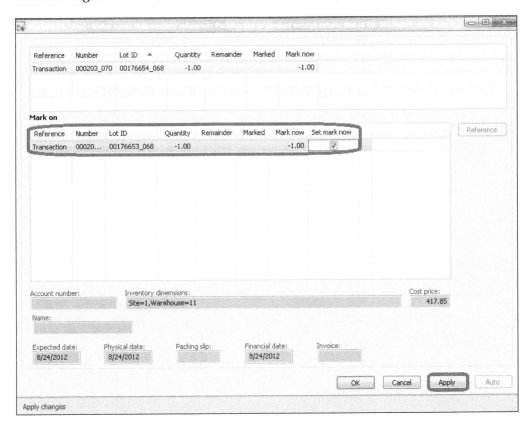

Summary

In this chapter, we covered the business model of inventory costing based on the business domain; the required configuration and setup of Microsoft Dynamics AX in the inventory management module, as well as the integration concepts with the general ledger to map business requirements. The difference between the physical and financial updates model of Microsoft Dynamics AX is the inventory transaction with marking functions, in addition to recalculations and closing processes.

In the next chapter, will cover the financial dimension and reporting practical practice in Microsoft Dynamics AX.

5
Exploring Financial Dimensions

One of the major objectives of an ERP implementation is to provide clear business insights that can provide support to the organization's top management in the decision-making process. This requires analyzing the numbers, understanding them clearly, and then being able to examine the same number from different perspectives. This requires a detailed structure to decide how an organization wants to analyze their numbers. This chapter will cover the following topics:

- Understanding the financial dimension concept
- Understanding the ledger account segmentation
- Posting types in Microsoft Dynamics AX
- Exploring dimension reporting

Understanding the financial dimension concept

The main source of financial reporting is the main accounts. The components of financial reporting are balance sheet, income statement, trial balance, cash flow, and so on. The normal scenario is that the main account's balances do not mean much when it comes to analysis. This is because it is a total of posted transactions' amount, and it is required to be able to dig down into this total breakdown. In other words, it provides us with information on how this amount is allocated, for example, among business units and departments. This allocation gives the lowest level of analysis to break down the same balance for a main account by more than one dimensional perspective.

The following diagram shows the financial dimension allocation for the main account:

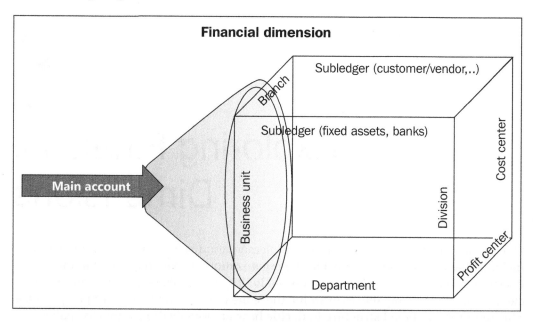

Financial dimensions provide us with a deeper analysis of the transactions posted on general ledger accounts, where it gives the controllership an analytical view of the transactions that occurred on the expenses account; for example, one can analyze the account balance according to the financial dimensions assigned to the main account.

Microsoft Dynamics AX 2012 financial dimension allows an organization to reach the lowest level of breakdown and analysis. There are three main standpoints to consider while discussing the financial dimension, which are shown in the following diagram. The first is the required breakdown analysis for each main account in the chart of accounts in order it to be utilized at the reporting level. The second is the controls and validations while data entry, in order to certify that the keyed-in transactions are allocated to the required dimensions before the transaction is posted; this directly affects the accuracy of reporting. The third is the reconciliation between the subledger and general ledger, and the ability to break down the balance using the subledger (customers, vendors, items, banks, and so on).

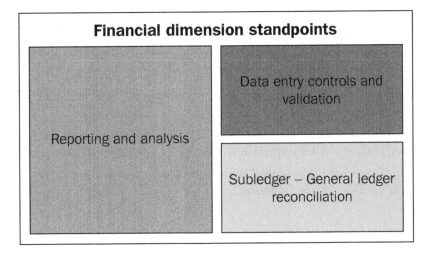

The role of the Microsoft Dynamics AX consultant is to clarify the best usage of financial dimensions to the concerned parties. The key process owners of ascertaining the financial dimensions' requirements are the **chief financial officer** (**CFO**) and the financial controller. The three main standpoints of financial dimension are summarized as follows:

- **Reporting and analysis**: This is used to identify reporting needs and data entry results
- **Data entry controls and validations**: This is used for data entry filtration
- **Subledger – General ledger reconciliation**: This is used for reconciliation of transactions between the subledger and the general ledger

The implementation team ascertains the financial dimensions' requirements during the analysis phase to understand what the business needs are at the reporting and analysis stage, and then identifies the required number of financial dimensions and how to utilize these dimensions.

 Microsoft Dynamics AX 2012 supports an unlimited number of financial dimensions.

According to the business domain, every business needs to build the structure of their chart of accounts and financial dimensions. They also need to identify which subledger should be tracked at the general ledger level. To build the structure of the chart of accounts and financial dimensions, follow the ensuing steps:

- Classify the required dimensions for each main account, whether it is mandatory or optional

- Categorize the financial dimensions that are interrelated and are dependent on each other to filter dimensions based on the previously selected value

- Categorize what intra-related dimensions are; these are not dependent on the previously selected dimension

 Microsoft Dynamics AX 2012 supports the use of the existing subledger master data to define financial dimensions.

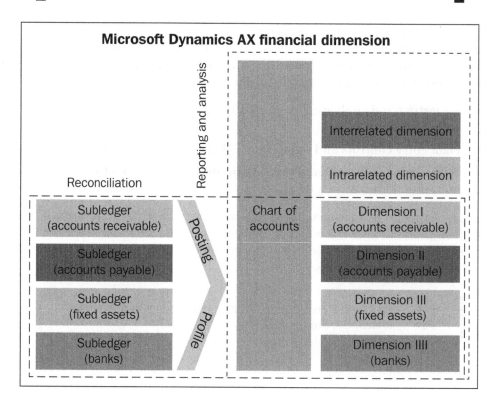

The heart of a financial dimension is the **Chart of accounts** as shown in the previous diagram. It should be carefully structured and set to the required dimension validation of each main account. It is important to consider this structure of the chart of accounts and dimensions' validation in the opening balance upload, as it will affect reporting and analysis in addition to an automatic transaction such as the exchange rate adjustment.

> Changing the financial dimension's structure and validation during operations should be wisely planned, evaluated, and executed as it may affect some historical transactions and some automatic transactions (for example, exchange rate adjustment, inventory adjustment, and settlement). It is recommended to apply it at the beginning of a month when all historical transactions, along with the old structure and validation, are closed.

Understanding the ledger account segmentation

The following section covers the newly introduced segmented ledger account entry in Microsoft Dynamics AX 2012 and the financial dimensions' assignment in a one-line voucher entry.

Segmented ledger accounts

Microsoft Dynamics AX 2012 introduced the segmented ledger account where the main account and the financial dimension are combined altogether in a single line. It gives more flexibility and control to the data that is entered than the previous versions.

The data entries are considered as the major sources of information quality. During the analysis phase, the implementation team exploring the reporting requirements, as well as the process owners and top management require reliable information, and this information is generated by the data entry. It is required to control the data entry to ensure the entered data is formatted in the correct way. The application consultant can fulfill these requirements to ensure the quality of data entry by performing the following tasks: default some values from the master data that are automatically populated in the transaction, by changing fields to be mandatory for reporting, and identifying the required financial dimensions, to the transaction level.

Microsoft Dynamics AX 2012 offers a very powerful entry mechanism which is built on the account structure. The segmented entry control is a function that simplifies data entry and controls the complex combination of accounts and financial dimensions.

It is a simple cheat-sheet window that gives the user hints on which segment should be entered, in addition to the lookup for this segment.

To access the general journal, navigate to **General ledger | Journal | General journal lines**. The following screenshot shows the simple cheat sheet in detail:

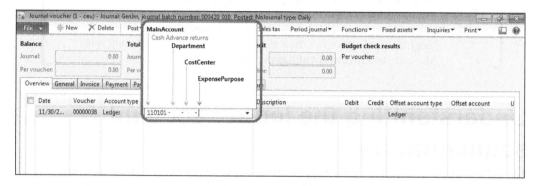

Financial dimensions entry

In this section, we will explore further enhancement of segmented entries that gives more flexibility to Microsoft AX 2012 to accommodate the one-line entry to allocate the segments. This was followed in previous versions of Microsoft Dynamics AX, where the default application assigned dimensions to both the sides (Debit and Credit), enforcing the use of double-line entries to work around this issue.

Microsoft AX 2012 covers this point completely. If an entry is created in a one-line style, the voucher created is that of a debit (vendor) or credit (bank) and requires the assigning of different segments. Here is a new feature where we will be able to assign different financial dimensions for **Account** and **Offset account**, as shown in the following screenshot:

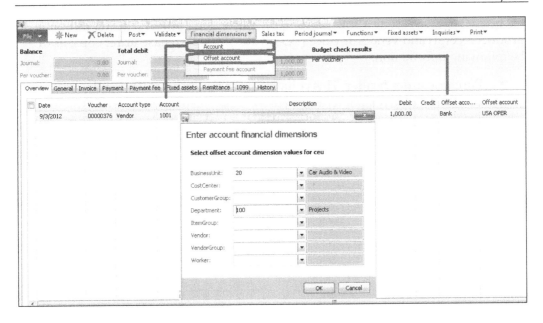

Financial dimension's posting mechanism in transaction documents

The posting of financial dimensions' in transaction documents (purchase order and sales order) has a specific mechanism that is complied with financial posting. Here, at the first posting stage (**Product receipt/Packing slip**), the entries are generated from the item posting profile; in other words, from the lines. And at the second posting stage (**Invoice**), the entries are generated from the header that reverses the first stage entry and generates the invoice entry from the header posting profile and the inventory posting profile.

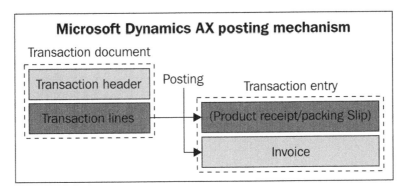

It is normal to assign some dimensions to the purchasing process during reception (product receipt) and vendor invoice (PO invoice). The **Purchase order** consists of the following information:

- **Purchase order header**: This contains information on assigning the vendor, their address, payment terms, method of payment, and financial dimension

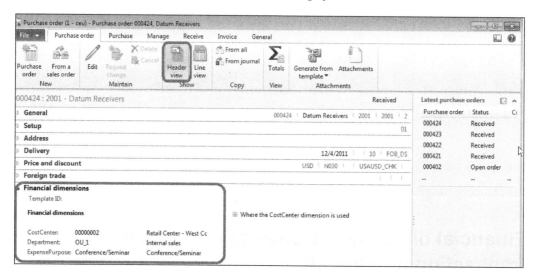

- **Purchase order lines**: This contains information on assigning the item, its quantity, price, and financial dimension

To access purchase order, navigate to **Procurement and sourcing | Common | Purchase orders | All purchase orders** as shown in the following screenshot:

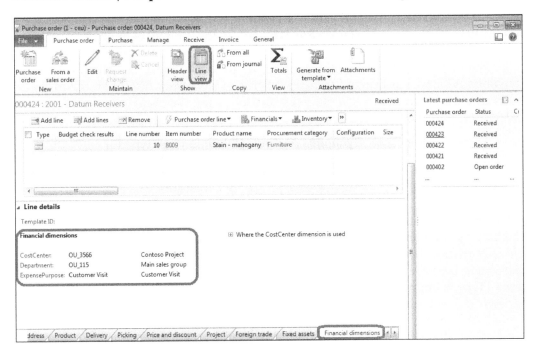

The autogenerated financial transactions of the purchase order are product receipt and invoice. The financial dimensions are automatically inherited from the purchase order form (**Purchase order header** and **Purchase order lines**).

The financial dimension's assignment to voucher entries has a certain mechanism; it should be addressed and communicated with the controllership to make him/her aware of this treatment. This mechanism is as follows:

- The generated voucher entry, which represents the product receipt, inherits the financial dimensions from **Purchase order lines**

- The generated voucher entry, which represents the invoice, inherits the financial dimensions from **Purchase order header**

Creating financial dimensions

There was an obstacle facing the implementation team in assigning master data to financial dimensions such as vendors, customers, fixed assets, items, and banks, and the best case scenario to tackle this is an automatic (online) assignment, in order to keep the integrity. The solution for this requirement is that it will either be maintained manually or by an automatic trigger (customization). Microsoft Dynamics AX 2012 has bridged this gap. Microsoft Dynamics AX 2012 has two types of financial dimensions as shown in the following diagram:

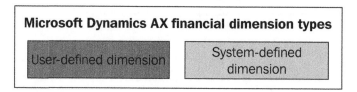

The first type is the user-defined dimension, which was used in Microsoft Dynamics AX 2009 to allow users to add an unlimited number of dimensions (business unit, cost center, purpose, profit center, and so on) as per the outcome of the analysis. The second type is the system-defined dimension that helps in assigning the master data to newly created dimensions, such as vendors, customers, fixed assets, and items.

The steps to create a new dimension are as follows:

1. Navigate to **General ledger | Setup | Financial dimensions**.

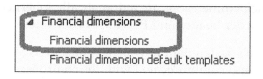

2. Navigate to **General ledger | Setup | Financial dimensions | Financial dimensions**.

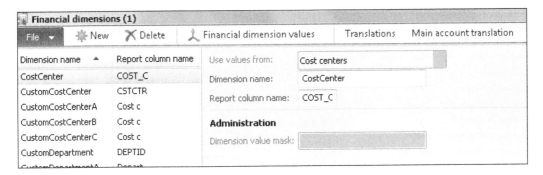

3. Create a new financial dimension.

4. Navigate to **General ledger | Setup | Financial dimensions | Financial dimensions | New** as shown in the following screenshot:

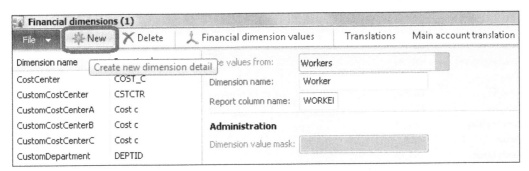

5. Select the dimension type.

6. If you want to add a user-defined dimension, select **<Custom dimension>** as shown in the following screenshot:

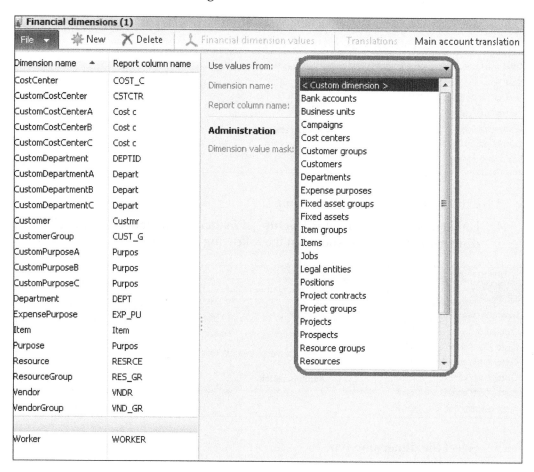

7. Enter the user-defined dimension list and configure the dimension value by its dates of activation and/or suspension by filling the **Active from**, **Active to**, and **Suspended** fields as shown in the following screenshot:

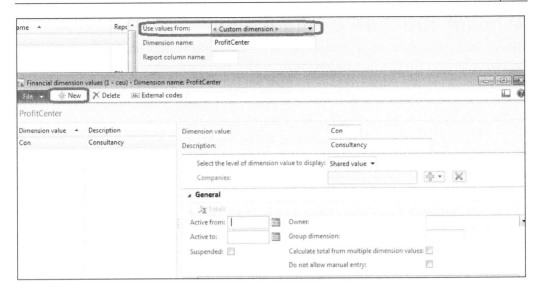

8. Select the subledger values, for example, **Customers**. Additionally, select the financial values called from the customer's master data and configure the dimension value by its dates of activation and/or suspension.

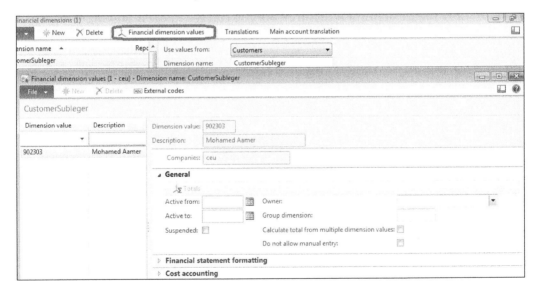

Account structure configuration

The account structure's configuration identifies the required dimensions for the main account. The account structure is attached to the company's ledger setup (*Chapter 1, Understanding the General Ledger*). As you can see in the following diagram, an account structure is a combination of the main account and financial dimensions:

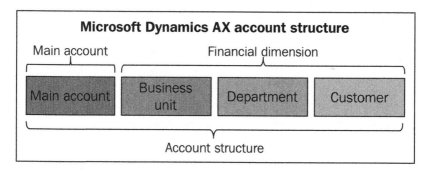

Microsoft Dynamics AX 2012 provides flexibility to add the account structure for main accounts with any combination of financial dimensions.

To configure the account structures, navigate to **General ledger | Setup | Chart of accounts | Configure account structures**. As you can see in the following screenshot, **Configure account structures** should be in the edit mode to be edited:

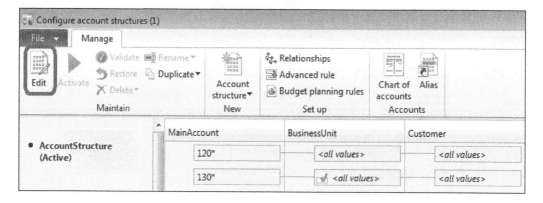

Add a segment (financial dimension) to the account structure that is already defined, whether user-defined or system-defined dimensions, by clicking on the **Add segment** option as shown in the following screenshot:

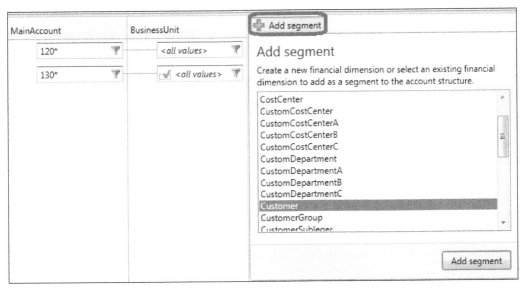

Microsoft Dynamics AX 2012 provides an option to identify the main account by identifying one specific account and/or a part of the main accounts. This is done by selecting **Specify which values are allowed** as shown in the following screenshot. This provides the availability to use the filtration option.

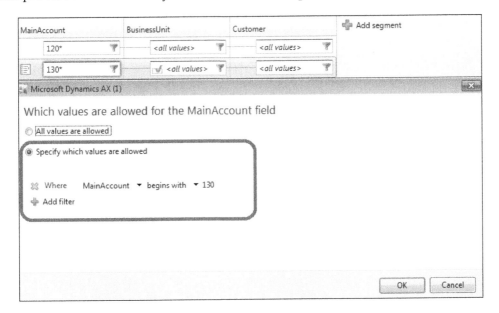

As you can see in the following screenshot, it is possible to arrange the order of the dimensions by moving the segments to the left or right, or right-click to move the segment:

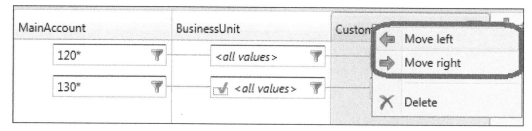

Accepting a blank (null) value in the dimension is possible. This feature is introduced in Microsoft Dynamics AX 2012, whether you accept a value or keep it blank, and it is allowed for users to leave the dimension blank as shown in the following screenshot:

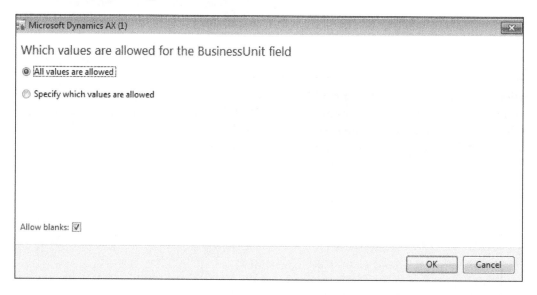

To apply the account structure configuration, it must be activated as shown in the following screenshot:

Posting types in Microsoft Dynamics AX

In Microsoft Dynamics AX, there are two ways to post transactions to the main account. The first type is through the posting profile that represents the integration point between the general ledger and subledger, and it generates the financial entries automatically according to the posting profile's setup. The second type is the journal entries that posts directly to the ledger accounts.

The posting profile concept

Posting profiles are the integration point between the subledger (fixed assets, accounts payable, inventory, banks, accounts receivable, project, and production) and the general ledger. It is a set of main accounts that are used to generate the automatic ledger entry in which a transaction has occurred. It is possible to select different main accounts for each type of subledger transactions. Microsoft Dynamics AX offers flexibility in the setting up of posting profiles. Posting could be on three different levels as follows:

- **All**: Any transaction occurring on any subledger (such as customers, vendors, items, and/or items) will be redirected to the main account, which is assigned to all customers, vendors, and/or items

- **Group B**: Any transaction for a particular customer, vendor, and/or item inherits the posting profile of the customer, vendor, and/or item group to which the customer, vendor, and/or item is assigned

- **Table**: Any transaction that occurs for a subledger, vendor, and/or item will be directed to the ledger account, which is assigned to the posting profile

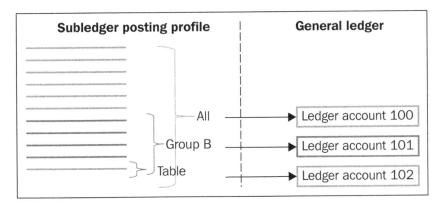

The common question during the design phase is which level out of **All**, **Group B**, and **Table** will dominate over the other levels. Customers can be assigned to a specific group, but in some exceptions, such as this one, the customer should be directed to another ledger account. The lowest-level of all is **Table,** which specifies the customer ID that will dominate over **Group B** and **All**.

The posting profile hierarchy in Microsoft Dynamics AX 2012 works as follows:

To access the posting profile, navigate to the following paths:

- For accounts payable posting profiles, navigate to **Accounts payable | Setup | Vendor posting profiles**

- For accounts receivable posting profiles, navigate to **Accounts receivable | Setup | Customer posting profiles**

- For inventory posting profile, navigate to **Inventory and warehouse management | Setup | Posting | Posting**

> The ledger accounts specified in the posting profile must not allow a manual entry to be created in the general ledger to preserve the integrity between the general ledger and subledger.

Journal posting

The journal model in Microsoft Dynamics AX is a journal header that contains voucher lines. Here the default data in the journal name (header) is copied to the voucher lines, such as currency and sales taxes, which can be changed in the voucher line. Every subledger has its own journal name based on the transaction type.

The voucher line can be a ledger account, vendor account, customer account, fixed asset, bank, or project. If the selected account is an option other than the ledger account, the subledger posting profile will direct the posting to the ledger account.

- **Journal posting controls**: The journal posting controls consist of embedded controls that cannot be changed or avoided. The voucher balance and other controls are basic setups for each journal name that can be applied at any time.

  - **Voucher balance and journal balance**: The basic accounting principle, which is a financial entry, must be balanced so that the debit side is equal to the credit side. Microsoft Dynamics AX prevents posting any transaction if there are any discrepancies between the transactions sides (debit/credit). This validation occurs on the voucher line as well as the journal.

- **Transaction date**: The balance voucher must be posted on the same date. Microsoft Dynamics AX applies the concept of one-line voucher entry and two-line entries. This control is validated if the entry appears on two lines.

- **Offset account**: Fixing an offset account on a specific journal will prevent users from changing or modifying the offset account on the voucher line; it can be a proposal and it may be changed at the transaction level.

- **Blocking the journal name**: During the daily operations on the journal entries in Microsoft Dynamics AX, whether these journals are related to the general ledger, fixed assets, accounts payable, accounts receivables, inventory journals movement, transfer journals, or bill of materials (BOM), it is normal to have more than one journal name under the same journal type. Each journal name serves a specific business transaction based on the business requirements gathered in the analysis phase. Microsoft Dynamics AX gives this control to a private user group in the journal name configuration. This prevents the use of this journal only for the appropriate user group.

- **Journal approvals**: Approval controls on general ledger journals are divided into two levels. The first level is the one step approval and second level is the workflow approval. The workflow approval requires an automatic batch job to run at a specific interval in order to make sure the approvers receive the documents that require approval.

  - **One step approval**: This is considered as a simple configuration for the journal's approvals, as it assigns a user group to be the approval group for a specific journal name.

  - **Workflow approval**: This approval needs to configure a workflow approval step. This gives you the flexibility to add a complex approval matrix that will be triggered if the condition occurs on the journal, so the workflow approval offers more control on journal posting.

To access the journal names, navigate to **General ledger | Journals | Journal names**.

Exploring dimension reporting

Overall, this chapter covers the financial dimension model from business and application angles. The required configuration for main accounts and the account structure directly affects the accuracy of the data entered by controlling the dimensions' selection and validation.

The following section will explore the financial dimension's reporting capabilities in trial balance and dimension statement.

Financial dimension sets

Financial dimension sets are the results of reporting the transactions based on financial dimensions. It can be a combination of more than one financial dimension. Financial dimension sets are initially designed, along with the designing of financial dimensions in the design phase, to accommodate the reporting perspective, and they can be extended during the operations.

As you can see in the following diagram, the financial dimension set is used as a focus point in reporting where it will be able to analyze numbers by one dimension focus or more than one focus:

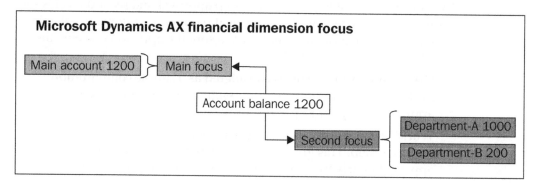

Identify the financial dimension set by selecting one or more dimensions from **Available financial dimensions** as an analyzing level as shown in the following screenshot:

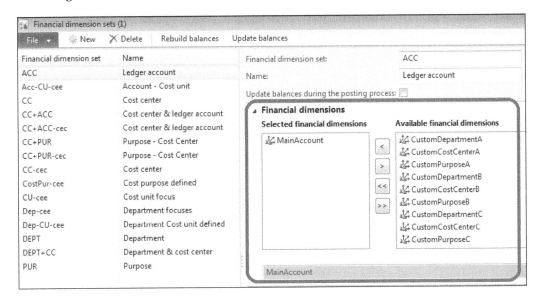

To access financial dimension sets, navigate to **General ledger | Setup | Financial dimension | Financial dimension sets**.

The trial balance is one of the major financial reports where it will be able to generate a transaction's trial balance for all the main accounts. In Microsoft Dynamics AX 2012, this report is converted to a form.

To access the trial balance, navigate to **General ledger | Common | Trial balance** as shown in the following screenshot:

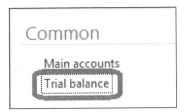

Identify the reporting date of the trial balance by entering the following dates:

- **From date**: In this field, enter the start date of the report date range
- **To date**: In this field, enter the end date of the report date range

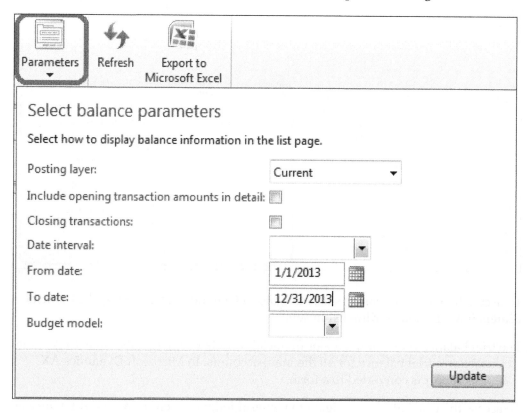

The date range of trial balance should be within one fiscal year Infolog message in the format "From date is in fiscal year 20XX. To date is in fiscal year 20XX. Dates must be in same fiscal year."

For example, "From date is in fiscal year 2010. To date is in fiscal year 2011. Dates must be in same fiscal year."

Identify **Financial dimension set** as a focus option as shown in the following screenshot:

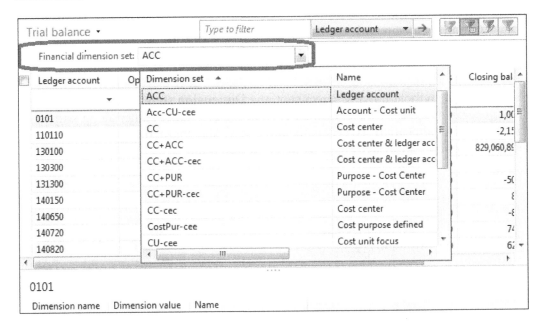

The **Trial balance** is broken down by the selected **Financial dimension set** as shown in the following screenshot:

The trial balance contains the following information:

- **Ledger account**: This shows the main account or the account structure dimension

- **Opening balance**: This shows the opening balance amount after closing the fiscal year

- **Debit**: This shows the transaction of the amount debited on that account (monthly movement)

- **Credit**: This shows the transaction of the amount credited on that account (monthly movement)

- **Closing balance**: This shows the closing balance for that account at the end; *date range = Net difference + Opening balance*

As you can see in the following screenshot, the **Dimension statement** is the most often generated report by the controller to examine the main balance along with the dimensions' allocation. To access the dimension statement, navigate to **General ledger | Reports | Transactions | Dimension statement**.

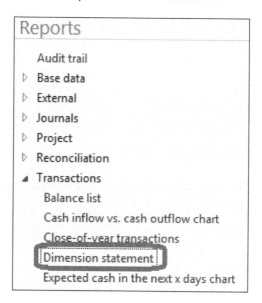

The financial dimensions' report filtration identifies the following parameters:

Parameter	Description
Primary financial dimension set	To select the primary financial dimension set for the report
Secondary financial dimension set	To select the secondary financial dimension set for the report
Date interval	To select the current date interval for the report
From date	To enter or select the start of the date range to print transactions for

Parameter	Description
To date	To enter or select the end of the date range to print transactions for
New page	Select this checkbox to insert a page break between each account
Posting layer	To select how the posting layer or posting layer combination should be included for the selected column, such as: • **Current**: This column will contain transactions that are included in the current posting layer • **Operations**: This column will contain transactions that are included in the **current** or **operations** posting layers • **Tax**: This column will contain transactions that are included in the **tax posting** layer • **Operations minus tax**: This column will contain the net transactions from the **operations posting** layer minus the **tax** posting layer • **Only operations**: This column will contain transactions that are included in the **operations** posting layer • **Only tax**: This column will contain transactions that are included in the **tax posting** layer • **Operations plus tax**: This column will contain transactions that are included in the **operations** or **tax posting** layers • **Total**: This column will contain transactions that are included in the **current**, **operations**, or **tax posting** layers
Include the opening transaction amounts in detail	Select this checkbox to exclude the opening transactions from the line of the report that lists the opening balance. Opening transactions are displayed in the report detail.
Closing transactions	Select this checkbox to display the closing transactions as transactions. Clear this checkbox to display the closing transactions in the closing balance in the summary form.

As you can see in the following screenshot, the dimension statement breaks down the account balance by department:

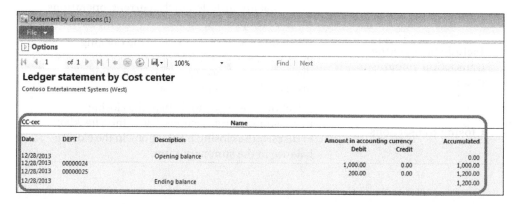

Summary

This chapter covers the business concept of the financial dimension, segmentation of ledger accounts. This chapter also covers Microsoft Dynamics AX posting profile types, journal posting and its controls, and exploring its financial dimensions reporting.

In the next chapter, we will explore financial reporting and analysis, along with planning reporting needs, information source blocks, and discovering Microsoft Dynamics AX reporting options.

6
Exploring Financial Reporting and Analysis

The main principles of reporting are the reliability of business information and the ability to get the right information at the right time for the right person. Reports that analyze ERP data in an expressive way represent the output of the ERP implementation. It is considered as the cream of the implementation and the next level of value that the solution stakeholders should target for. This ultimate outcome results from building all reports based on a single point of information. This chapter will cover the following topics:

- Planning reporting needs for ERP
- Understanding information technology value chain
- Understanding Microsoft Dynamics AX information source blocks
- Discovering Microsoft Dynamics AX reporting
- Reporting options
- Reporting currency

Planning reporting needs for ERP

The Microsoft Dynamics AX implementation teamwork should challenge the management's reporting needs in the analysis phase of the implementation, with a particular focus on exploring the data required to build reports. These data requirements should then be cross-checked with the real data entry activities that end users will execute to ensure that business users will get vital information from the reports.

On several projects, there are no well-defined reports except the financial reports (trial balance, income statement, and balance sheet) that are in place during analysis. Later, for live operations on such projects, the implementation teamwork determines the need for more data and starts chasing the required information inside the application by completing the missing information, fields, and/or redesigning the data entry process. This may lead to an increase in the data entry time due to additional steps for data validations and the surprise discovery that there are not enough end user resources to execute the updated requirements. So, there should be a balance between the sum of required data entry values that directly affect the reporting quality and the total number of end user resources that perform the data entry process.

Another word of caution: the solution architect may recognize during the operation that some transactions are performed by one end user but typically, these transactions are performed by two or three end users to attain the segregation of duties and control. For example, in the procurement cycle, there is one user who creates the inventory item, purchase order, and reception. But normally these transactions are performed by three different users. In this kind of resource-constrained situation, the segregation of duties and control concepts are breached and the ERP solution is negatively impacted for the end users and key users. In these situations, the root cause of the concern is not the functionalities of ERP but the lack of allocated resources.

The two other important models of reporting are pulling and pushing reports. Pulling of reports refers to the active requesting of reports by operational managers for the lowest transactional level, such as purchasing, warehousing, sales, marketing, and financial entries. The middle management layer will pull reports to serve procurement, commercial/sales, and controllership.

Pushing of reports refers to the Business Intelligence (BI) capabilities that serve the top management, such as offering KPIs, balance score cards, and analytics/comparison views. The various reporting levels of Microsoft Dynamics AX are shown in the following diagram:

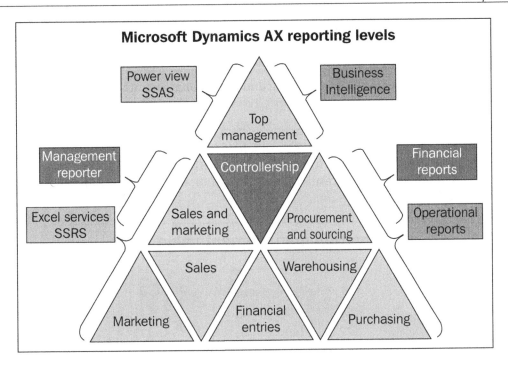

Microsoft Dynamics AX 2012 R2 and the supporting Microsoft technology stack offers a diversity of reporting capabilities, including ad hoc reports for the transactional level, developed by Microsoft Excel 2013, Excel Services, and Microsoft **SQL Server Analysis Services (SSAS)**. The Microsoft Dynamics **Management reporter** offers the controllership, in the middle management the facility to create and run financial reports. For the BI solutions built for Microsoft Dynamics AX, customers should begin with Excel Power View, SSAS, and PerformancePoint Services in SharePoint. The different levels of management are as follows:

- **Operational Management**: The operational managers are involved in monitoring the performance of each business unit and managing employees
- **Middle Management**: The middle managers are focused with internal firm performance including revenues and costing management, resource allocation, and the development of short-term plans
- **Top Management**: The top managers are focused on business strategic decisions that affect long-term plans, future performance, and the overall firm's objectives

Understanding the information technology value chain

In this section, we will explore reporting and data management in ERP from the management information system perspective with its dependent layers.

The model of a management information system is most applicable to a businesses' **Information Technology (IT)** manager or **Chief Information Officer (CIO)**. Business owners likely don't care as much about the specifics as long as these aspects of the solution deliver the required results. The information management value chain is shown in the following diagram:

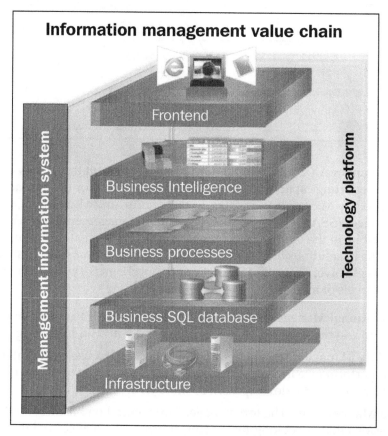

ERP implementations in enterprise projects are multipart for success. The most common element is addressing business requirements at all enterprise levels, from basic IT infrastructure through user interface technology.

Infrastructure

Infrastructure is vital and ensures the reliability of the solution, assuring the availability of daily business operations. It must also be able to sustain an agreed level of uptime.

Hardware sizing depends on elements as well as number of transactions, users, locations, and the available connectivity for each location. The infrastructure must also meet the architectural requirements of the servers that will ride the application, database, and reporting.

Beyond the live production planning environment, each company should consider building at least three different environments. The first is a development environment for testing customizations and new functionalities. The second is a training environment that is a replication of the live environment and can accept tested updates from the development environment. The third is a live production environment for live transactions. It is similarly important to consider clustering and load balancing.

Having a single reporting server improves the reporting performance with SQL BI reporting or **SQL Server Reporting Services** (**SSRS**). Furthermore, there are automatic batch jobs for notifications, alerts, and running special processes that set more load on the application server. So assigning these batch jobs to a separate server is favored. Depending on the industry, external access to Microsoft Dynamics AX can have an important impact on server performance. For example, for external access from customers and vendors, a retail business should consider an integrated e-commerce solution with Microsoft Dynamics AX.

Database management

The relational database (Microsoft SQL Server) that stores all the ERP-related transactions is known as **Online Transactional Processing** (**OLTP**). For BI reporting with a SQL Server, SSAS can store the aggregations, measures, and dimensions; resulting in higher performance in querying reports. It is also important to consider backup and restore strategies.

Reports from Microsoft Dynamics AX are based on the SSRS approach that has been standardized with Microsoft Dynamics AX 2012.

Business processes

The comprehensive business processes will reflect the data requirements. The design of a business process should identify the data owner and where and when the data was captured.

Business processes are transformed into business functions in Microsoft Dynamics AX. The applied access rights for users' security ensure the segregation of duties, data ownership, and accuracy of data validation. Similarly, the approval matrix in a workflow will define the control mechanisms in the business processes, such as the required management approvals.

Business Intelligence

It is often useful to analyze and measure company business results against industry benchmarks and best practices as a technique to develop the most valuable indicators and reports.

The richness of Power View and Excel Services gives Microsoft Dynamics AX 2012 Enterprise Portal significant power to do analysis and increase business insights more than any earlier release.

Frontend

The frontend pinpoints the devices that the organization will need to access the applications that are being used. The most commonly-used device in many organizations is still the laptop. More widespread access from numerous locations over the Internet may require more planning for mobile devices (cellular phones, handheld devices, and tablets). For example, Microsoft has introduced Microsoft Business Analyzer for Windows 8 that gives access to the high-level reports of charts for Microsoft Dynamics AX.

Understanding Microsoft Dynamics AX information source blocks

In this section, we will explore the information sources that eventually determine the strategic value of BI reporting and analytics. These are divided into three blocks. The first block is the detailed transaction level, the second is business intelligence, and third is executive decisions. These three blocks are explained in the following sections.

Detailed transactions block

At its roots, BI depends on capturing accurate transactional data from business processes at the first level of detail and transforming these processes into a regular flow of meaningful entries in an ERP solution, such as Microsoft Dynamics AX. Application consultants should consider the reports that are required by the customers and certify that the required data points are captured through the recording process for daily transactions. Whenever possible, the application consultant has a responsibility to also challenge the business process owners about the process, as it relates to using the data to make changes to optimize the business. The following diagram shows the detailed **Transactions** block:

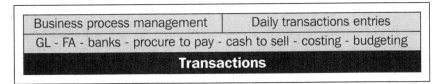

In some projects, consultants split their attention between business process workshops during business requirement gathering in the analysis phase and the establishment of the data structure in forms during the design phase. It is vital to document the business process, including the start point, end point, comprehensive steps of the process (if needed), the data path in each step, and exceptional cases for each process. On the other hand, the forms are a transformation of the business processes into the real work activities of employees (fields, grids, buttons, multiple selection, and so on).

The main processes that should be addressed in a typical ERP implementation include banks, fixed assets, procure to pay, cash to sell, costing, and budgeting with the general ledger integration for each.

Business Intelligence block

BI is the second block in the information hierarchy that uses the raw data of transactions to provide valuable information to different levels of the organization. BI adds a layer of aggregation on transactions and makes it possible to create a comparative analysis for key measures such as actual versus budget.

The consultant should identify the measures needed and how they will be utilized from the transactional level. These measures are raw numbers aggregated from specific fields that result from a definite process or a combination of business processes.

Measures need to be informative—not just as raw numbers but as a source for analysis at the management level. The consultant should identify the analytic dimensions as well as the dimensions needed by the process owner to analyze numbers. The most common example is sales revenue, which can be analyzed by dimensions such as customer segmentations, geographical locations, warehouses, and customer demographics. The following diagram shows the **BI** block:

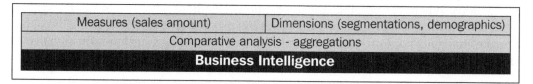

Now that we have seen the importance of the structure of reporting blocks based on the business processes and daily transaction data, it is worth exploring the common scenarios that consultants may face when the reporting requirements cannot be met by the data that is being captured. This missing data would lead a consultant to revisit the business process that includes entry of daily transactions, and identify a need for cleansing of historical data, which may be leading to the loss of some information.

Executive decisions block

The third block in the information source is the **Executive** decision support, where all the information is summarized and numbers are transformed into **KPIs**, **Indicators**, **Analytic Views**, and **Dashboard**. The following diagram shows the **Executive decisions** block:

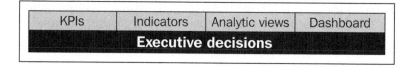

Executives do not have the luxury of time to drill down into all the comprehensive reports. They need a bird's eye view of the overall enterprise performance to support them in taking critical business decisions. With the right lower-level data, the ERP solution should be demonstrating its worth as a true decision support system that offers this visibility.

The conclusion is that when implementing Microsoft Dynamics AX solution, there is no reliable information for executives without a solid BI platform that is based on a well-defined ERP. The ERP absorbs business processes, such as the daily transactions entered by workers, with a high-level of clarity.

Discovering Microsoft Dynamics AX reporting options

The following section covers Microsoft Dynamics AX reporting options. The reporting options are inquiry forms and SSRS reports.

Reporting options

Reporting in Microsoft Dynamics AX can be generated through two approaches; the first is inquiry forms and the second is predesigned standard reports as shown in the following diagram:

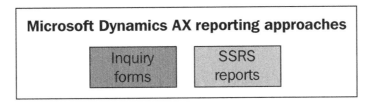

Inquiry forms

Inquiry forms are used for fast and easy reporting of transactions, where the transactions are listed. Advanced filtration gives the facility to reduce the inquiry results to a number of specific results. If it is required that you show all the transactions, don't identify any filter.

As you can see in the following screenshot, the advanced filtration and sorting functionalities are available in all AX 2012 screens by clicking on the ⬛ button or pressing *CTRL + F3*:

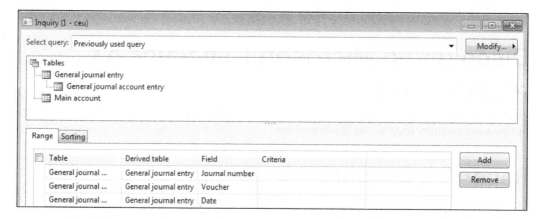

As you can see in the following screenshot, you can save a query and add new tables to a data source in advanced filtration by right-clicking on the **Tables** section.

- **1:n**: This represents the relation of one-to-many
- **n:1**: This represents the relation of many-to-one

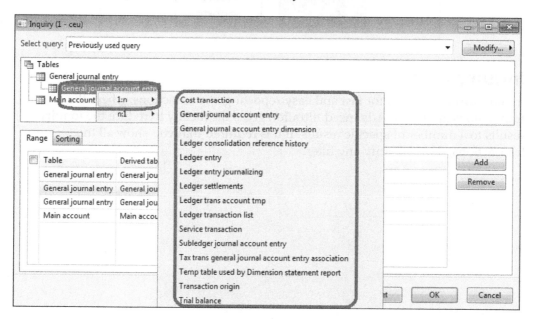

Under **Range**, we will be able to add tables that are available in the data source as shown in the following screenshot:

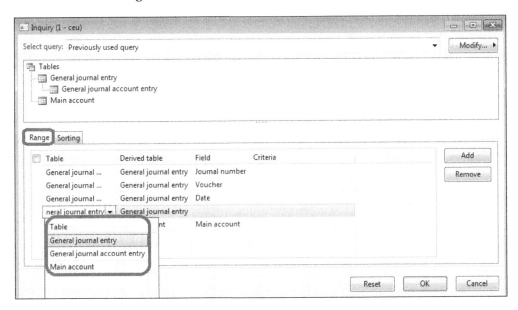

As you can see in the following screenshot, the **Field** column will be used for filtration and the **Criteria** column to identify values that are to be the base of the filtration:

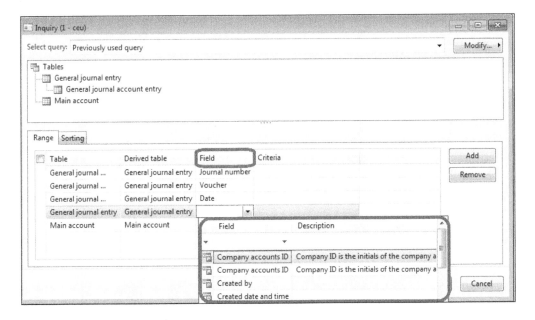

The inquiry will result in a standard Microsoft Dynamics AX 2012 form, and you can use the quick information on the transaction by mouse over in addition to the personalization options as shown in the following screenshot:

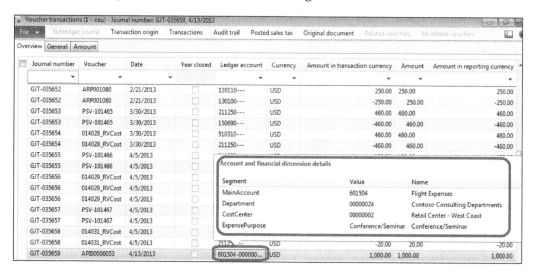

After the form generation, we can use wild character filtration by pressing *Ctrl + G* and the following screenshot appears:

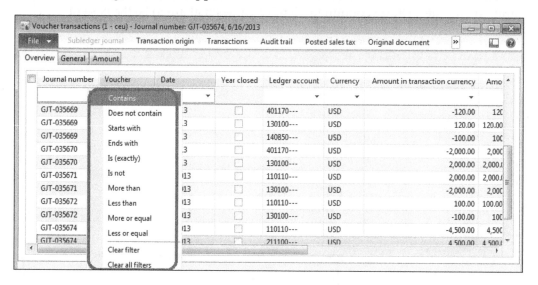

The wild characters used for filtration in grids are as follows:

*: Any character match

?: Must have character

..: From to range

!: Does not have

!A*: Does not begin with

>/<: Greater/Less than

,: Values and other

SSRS reports

SSRS reports are used to generate reports in the document format to be printed for filing, which are used as official supporting documents in the company's template or as external official documents. The normal advanced filtration is the base of SSRS report generation and can sort report results. We can also use the tables that are in the data source, specify the fields that will be the base of the sorting, and the available sorting option, either **Ascending** or **Descending**.

For the ledger transaction list, navigate to **General ledger | Reports | Transactions | Ledger transaction list** and the following screenshot will appear:

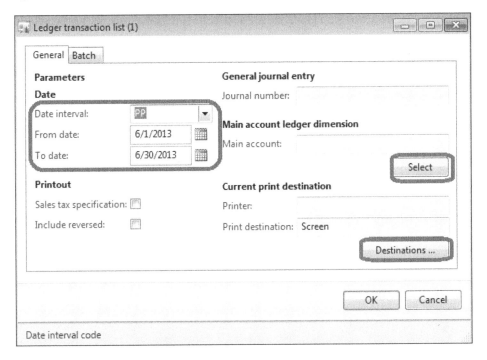

After completing the selection criteria, navigate to the **Sorting** tab to identify the report sorting as shown in the following screenshot:

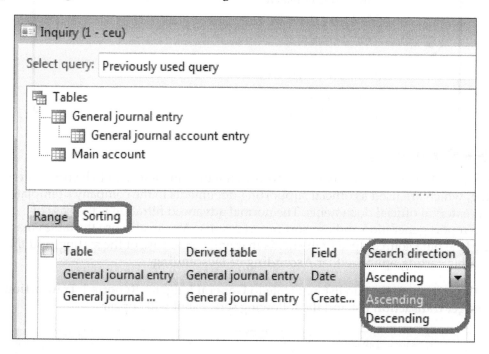

In the **Print destination settings**, identify the location of report printing, that is, the **Screen**, **Printer**, or **E-mail**. Also select the **File format**, which can be **Microsoft Excel**, **HTML**, **PDF**, **CSV**, and so on as shown in the following screenshot:

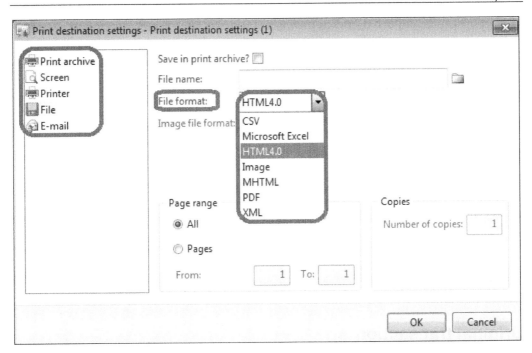

As you can see in the following screenshot, the generated report is based on SSRS, which gives more flexibility to the report layout:

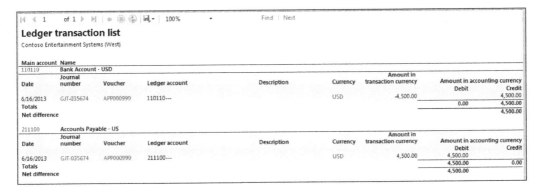

The report can be exported after report generation by the export function as shown in the following screenshot:

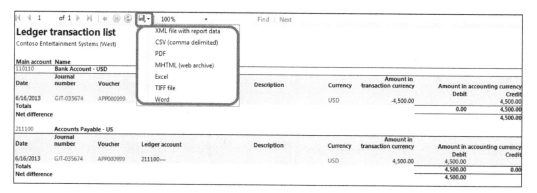

There are three major preferences for financial reporting that should be familiar to Microsoft Dynamics AX users, which are original transaction, original document, and audit trail.

Original transaction

The **Transaction origin** function fetches the transaction entries that are posted to the general ledger and their effect on the subledgers as well.

The **Transaction origin** function can be performed to fetch any transaction entry. It is commonly used when you need to identify the subledger affected by this entry.

For voucher transactions, navigate to **General ledger | Inquiries | Voucher transactions** as shown in the following screenshot:

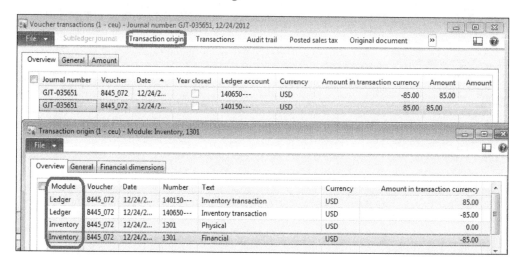

Original document

The **Original document** function fetches the transaction entries posted in the general ledger and reaches the original document that generated this entry.

As shown in the following screenshot, the **Original document** function gives the facility to reach the original transaction document regardless of whether it is a general ledger entry, sales order, purchase order, and so on:

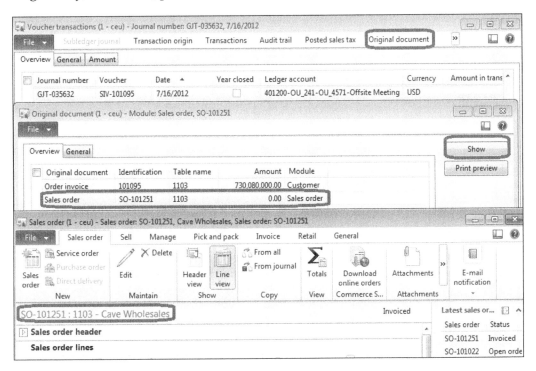

Audit trail

The **Audit trail** function fetches the transaction entries posted in the general ledger and reports who posted it and when. It gives the facility to show who posted the transaction, when, and from which document type. The following screenshot shows the **Audit trail** option of Microsoft Dynamics AX:

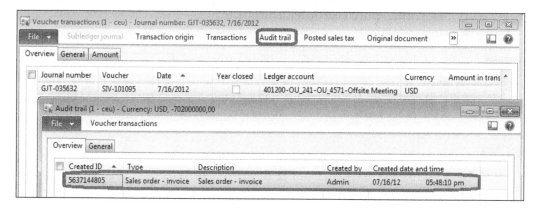

 There is a creation date and time that represents the actual date of posting the transaction was posted. However, this is not the financial posting date, which may be different from the creation date and time.

If the report's source is cube database or database warehouse (which replicate once a day from the transactional database at midnight (12:00AM)), and if a user posts a transaction in the previous date (session date for example, on June 30), then the report results will not be accurate if it is generated on July 01, the replication is not performed, and this transaction is not included in the previous replication. It will be included with effect from the next replication that will take place on July 02 (12:00).

Reporting currency

Companies report their transactions in a specific currency that is known as **accounting currency** or **local currency**. It is normal to post transactions in a different currency, and this amount of money is translated to the home currency using the current exchange rate. This is a business need in enterprises that operate in a multicountry environment; each subsidiary has its local reporting currency and at the same time, there should be a specific secondary reporting currency. All the transactions are translated into the reporting currency using the exchange rate.

To access reporting currency, navigate to **General ledger** | **Setup** | **Ledger** and the following screenshot will appear:

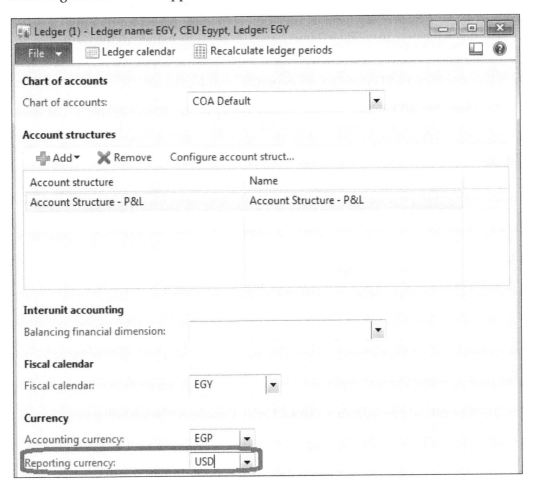

Autoreports

The autoreport wizard is a user-friendly tool. The end user can easily generate a report starting from every form in Microsoft Dynamics AX. The autoreport wizard helps the user to create a report based on the information in the form and save this report.

In this example, we will create an autoreport for vendor details.

1. Open the **All vendor** list page by navigating to **Accounts payable | Common | Vendors | All vendors** as shown in the following screenshot:

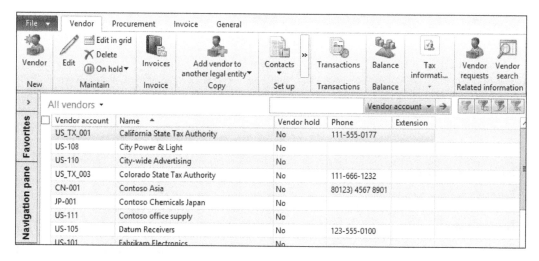

2. Navigate to **File | Print | Print... Ctrl + P** as shown in the following screenshot:

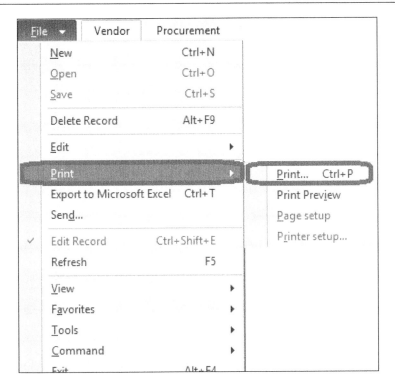

As you can see in the following screenshot, the **Autoreport** dialog box will pop up and here you can load a saved report or create a new report:

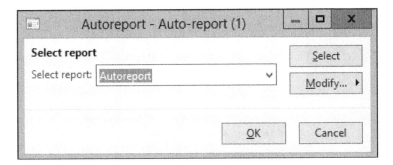

3. To create a new report, click on **Modify** and select **New** as shown in the following screenshot:

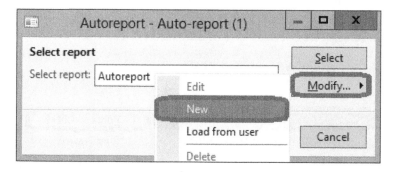

4. The **Autoreport Wizard** will pop up and then click on **Next** as shown in the following screenshot:

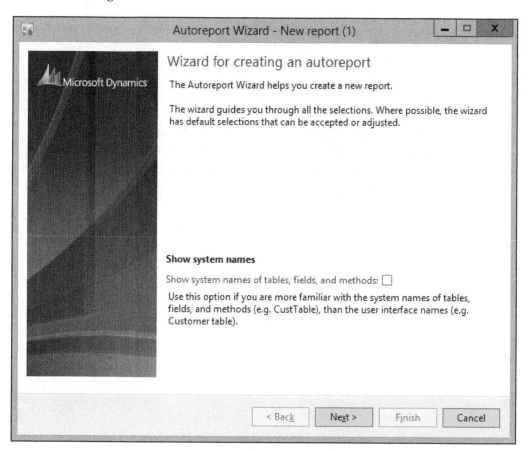

5. Enter the report name under the **Name** field and click on **Next**.

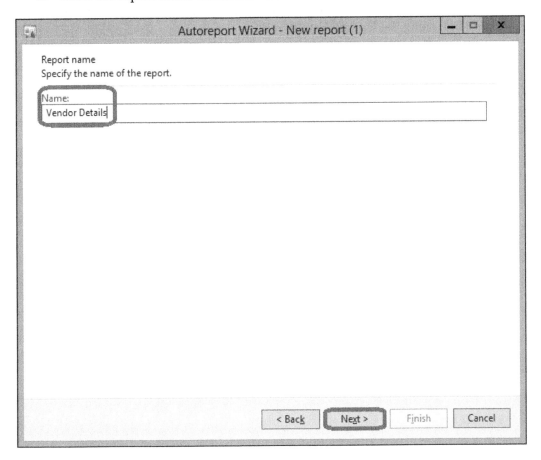

6. Select the report fields from the **Available fields** section using the left and right arrow buttons, and arrange the fields through the **Selected fields** section using the **Up** and **Down** buttons.

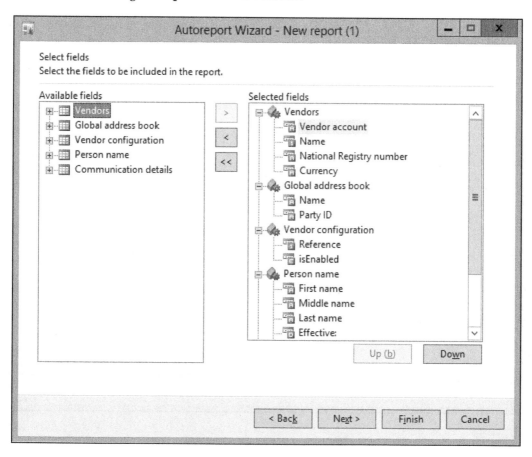

7. Specify the report template by selecting **Report layout template** and **Table style template**.

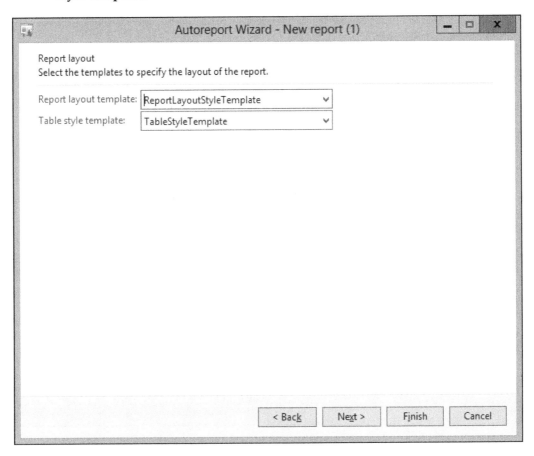

8.   Click on **Finish** to close **Autoreport Wizard**.

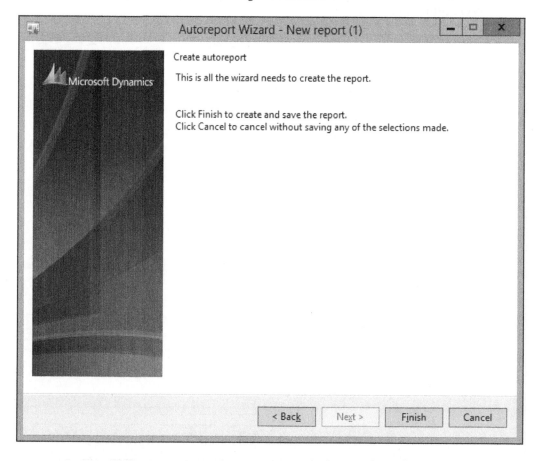

9.   To generate the saved report, navigate to **File | Print | Print and Select report name** and click on **OK**.

Summary

In this chapter, we have covered financial reporting from planning to consideration of reporting levels. We also covered important points that affect reporting quality.

We also learned about the reporting possibilities in Microsoft Dynamics AX such as inquiry forms and SSRS reports.

Index

journal posting controls
   journal approvals 111
   journal balance 110
   journal name, blocking 111
   offset account 111
   transaction date 111
   voucher balance 110

L

ledger reconciliation 48
Liquidity account 71
local currency. *See* **reporting currency**

M

Main account cash flow forecast 77
Main account category 11, 12
main account
   about 70
   account administration, using 16-18
   Debit/credit controls 13
   nontransactional accounts, using 10
   posting validation, using 19
   transactional accounts, using 8
Measures 128
Microsoft Dynamics AX
   autoreport 140-146
   journal posting 110, 111
   posting profile 109, 110
   reporting currency 138
   reporting options 129
Microsoft Dynamics AX 2012
   financial dimension types 102
Microsoft Dynamics AX information
   source blocks
   BI block 127, 128
   detailed transactions block 127
   Executive decisions block 128

N

New page parameter 117
nontransactional accounts
   reporting 11
   Totals 10

O

offset account 111
one step approval 111
Online Transactional Processing
   (OLTP) 125
opening balance
   about 26
   best practices 27
   elements 26
   execution 28-30
   planning and designing phase 28
   validation 30
Original document function 137

P

physical and financial update 87
physical update 87
planning and designing phase 28
Posting layer parameter 117
posting profile
   about 109, 110
   accessing 110
posting type 22, 23
posting validation
   currency control 19, 20
   posting type 22, 23
   user control 21, 22
Primary financial dimension set
   parameter 116
product dimension group 82, 83
profit and loss accounts 8
purchase order cash flow forecast 72, 73

R

reporting currency 138
reporting needs
   planning, for ERP 121-123
reporting options
   Audit trail function 138
   inquiry forms 129-132
   SSRS reports 133-136

S

Secondary financial dimension set
      parameter 116
segmented ledger account 97, 98
shared financial data 24, 25
SQL Server Analysis Services. *See* SSAS
SQL Server Reporting Services. *See* SSRS
SSAS 123
SSRS 125
SSRS reports
  about 133-136
  Original document function 137
  Transaction origin function 136
status activation
  about 46
  options 47
storage dimension group 83
system-defined dimension 102

T

To date parameter 117
Totals 10
tracking dimension group 84
transactional accounts
  balance accounts 8
  profit and loss accounts 8
transaction currency 48
transaction date 111
transaction documents
  financial dimension, posting 99-101
Transaction origin function 136
trial balance 115, 116

U

user control 21, 22
user-defined dimension 102

V

Validation list button 20
Vendor expenditure management
  about 60
  accounts payable 60
  procurement and sourcing 60
voucher balance 110

W

workflow approval 111

Thank you for buying
Microsoft Dynamics AX 2012
Financial Management

About Packt Publishing

Packt, pronounced 'packed', published its first book "Mastering phpMyAdmin for Effective MySQL Management" in April 2004 and subsequently continued to specialize in publishing highly focused books on specific technologies and solutions.

Our books and publications share the experiences of your fellow IT professionals in adapting and customizing today's systems, applications, and frameworks. Our solution based books give you the knowledge and power to customize the software and technologies you're using to get the job done. Packt books are more specific and less general than the IT books you have seen in the past. Our unique business model allows us to bring you more focused information, giving you more of what you need to know, and less of what you don't.

Packt is a modern, yet unique publishing company, which focuses on producing quality, cutting-edge books for communities of developers, administrators, and newbies alike. For more information, please visit our website: www.packtpub.com.

About Packt Enterprise

In 2010, Packt launched two new brands, Packt Enterprise and Packt Open Source, in order to continue its focus on specialization. This book is part of the Packt Enterprise brand, home to books published on enterprise software – software created by major vendors, including (but not limited to) IBM, Microsoft and Oracle, often for use in other corporations. Its titles will offer information relevant to a range of users of this software, including administrators, developers, architects, and end users.

Writing for Packt

We welcome all inquiries from people who are interested in authoring. Book proposals should be sent to author@packtpub.com. If your book idea is still at an early stage and you would like to discuss it first before writing a formal book proposal, contact us; one of our commissioning editors will get in touch with you.

We're not just looking for published authors; if you have strong technical skills but no writing experience, our experienced editors can help you develop a writing career, or simply get some additional reward for your expertise.

Implementing Microsoft Dynamics AX 2012 with Sure Step 2012

ISBN: 978-1-849687-04-1   Paperback: 234 pages

Get to grips with AX 2012 and learn a whole host of tips and tricks to ensure project success

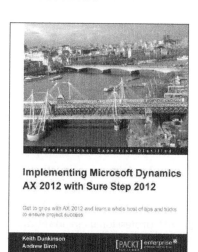

1. Get the confidence to implement AX 2012 projects effectively using the Sure Step 2012 Methodology

2. Packed with practical real-world examples as well as helpful diagrams and images that make learning easier for you

3. Dive deep into AX 2012 to learn key technical concepts to implement and manage a project

Microsoft Dynamics GP 2013 Cookbook

ISBN: 978-1-849689-38-0   Paperback: 348 pages

Over 110 immediately usable and effective recipes to solve real-world Dynamics GP problems

1. Understand the various tips and tricks to master Dynamics GP, and improve your system's stability in order to enable you to get work done faster

2. Discover how to solve real world problems in Microsoft Dynamics GP 2013 with easy-to-understand and practical recipes

3. Access proven and effective Dynamics GP techniques from authors with vast and rich experience in Dynamics GP

Please check **www.PacktPub.com** for information on our titles

**Building Dashboards with
Microsoft Dynamics GP 2013
and Excel 2013**

ISBN: 978-1-849689-06-9   Paperback: 268 pages

Creating, validating, and transforming XML
documents with Oracle's IDE

1. Build a dashboard using Excel 2013 with
    information from Microsoft Dynamics GP 2013

2. Make Excel a true business intelligence tool with
    charts, sparklines, slicers, and more

3. Utilize PowerPivot's full potential to create even
    more complex dashboards

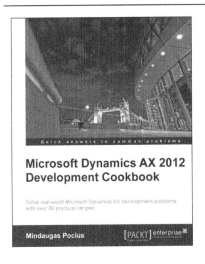

**Microsoft Dynamics AX 2012
Development Cookbook**

ISBN: 978-1-849684-64-4   Paperback: 372 pages

Easily build powerful dashboards with Microsoft
Dynamics GP 2013 and Excel 2013

1. Develop powerful, successful Dynamics AX
    projects with efficient X++ code with this book
    and eBook

2. Proven recipes that can be reused in numerous
    successful Dynamics AX projects

3. Covers general ledger, accounts payable,
    accounts receivable, project modules and
    general functionality of Dynamics AX

Please check **www.PacktPub.com** for information on our titles

CPSIA information can be obtained at www.ICGtesting.com
Printed in the USA
LVOW03s1224040114
368037LV00012B/419/P